KENNETH D. WALTERS

Moving Beyond Overthinking In Relationships

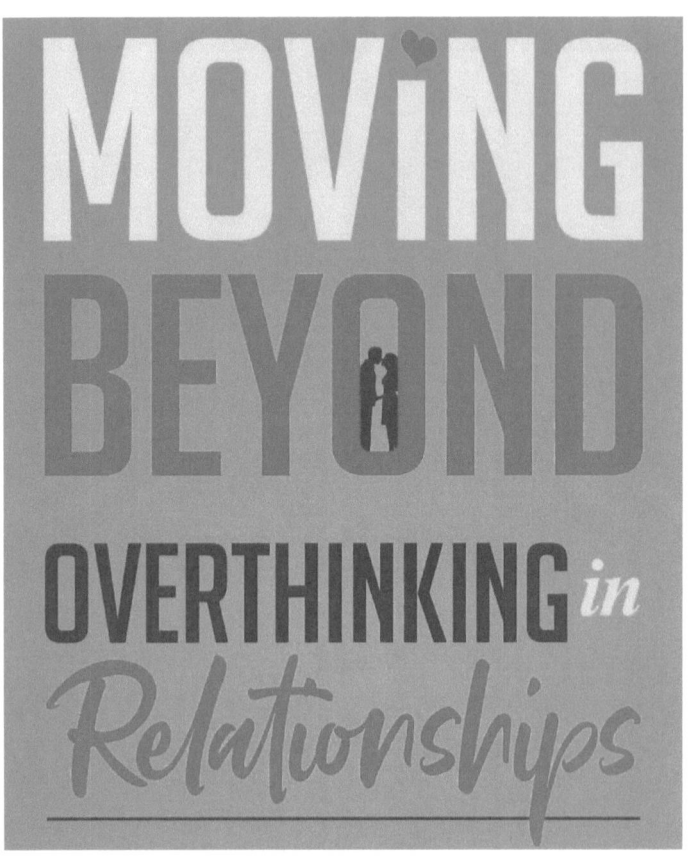

Moving Beyond Overthinking in Relationships

Navigate Anxiety Triggers,
Thereby Cultivating Authentic, Trusting, and
Worry-Free Connections Grounded in Honesty

Part of the
Thriving Relationships Series

Moving Beyond Overthinking in Relationships

Navigate Anxiety Triggers,
Thereby Cultivating Authentic, Trusting, and
Worry-Free Connections Grounded in Honesty

By Kenneth D Walters

✓|UNIQUELY MARK PUBLISHING

Uniquely Mark Publishing
Greenville, SC

© Copyright Kenneth D. Walters 2023 - All rights reserved.

The content contained within this book may not be reproduced, duplicated or transmitted without direct written permission from the author or the publisher.

Under no circumstances will any blame or legal responsibility be held against the publisher, or author, for any damages, reparation, or monetary loss due to the information contained within this book, either directly or indirectly. You are responsible for your own choices, actions, and results.

9 8 7 6 5 4 3 2 1

Legal Notice:

This book is copyright protected. This book is only for personal use. You cannot amend, distribute, sell, use, quote or paraphrase any part, or the content within this book, without the consent of the author or publisher.

Disclaimer Notice:

Please note the information contained within this document is for educational and entertainment purposes only. All effort has been executed to present accurate, up to date, and reliable, complete information. No warranties of any kind are declared or implied. Readers acknowledge that the author is not engaging in the rendering of legal, financial, medical or professional advice. The content within this book has been derived from various sources. Please consult a licensed professional before attempting any techniques outlined in this book.

By reading this document, the reader agrees that under no circumstances is the author responsible for any losses, direct or indirect, which are incurred as a result of the use of the information contained within this document, including, but not limited to, — errors, omissions, or inaccuracies.

Table of Contents

PREFACE 10
INTRODUCTION 13
   TIPS ON HOW TO EFFECTIVELY LEARN FROM THIS BOOK............................ 26
VIEW OVERTHINKING AS A DILEMMA, ... 28
NOT A DEFINITION 28
   A DEFINITION OF OVERTHINKING 29
   SOMETHING TO THINK ABOUT 32
   DETRIMENTAL MENTAL TRANSITION 33
   STRESS ON YOUR BODY AND BEHAVIOR 34
   TRAUMATIC EVENTS AND PERFECTIONISM 36
   TIME FOR A LITTLE LEVITY 42
   THE SCIENCE BEHIND OVERTHINKING 43
   OVERTHINKING'S EFFECT ON RELATIONSHIPS 47
   THE BLAME GAME CYCLE 50
   THE SELF-PITY CYCLE 50
   THE WORRY CYCLE 51
   THE CONTROL FREAK CYCLE 51
   THE DOUBT TRIP CYCLE 52
   A FAITH-BASED PERSPECTIVE ON OVERTHINKING 52
   A PERSONAL NOTE FROM THE AUTHOR 58
STOP TRYING TO READ SMOKE SIGNALS 62
   CURIOSITY 67
   PATIENCE 69
   CONTENTMENT 71
   S-L-O-W—SEE YOUR THOUGHTS 75
   S-**L**-O-W—LABEL THE THOUGHTS 79
      FACT OR PSEUDO-FACT 84
      OVERTHINKING CYCLES 88
   S-L-**O**-W—OPEN TO THE PRESENT 92
   S-L-O-**W**—WELCOME THE UNKNOWN 96
   THE BIG PICTURE OF SLOW 102

GET OFF THE RUMINATION ROLLERCOASTER 104
- Discover Your Triggers 106
- Avoiding Triggering Environments 111
- Mindset Triggers 114
- Showing Gratitude 124

GIVE THE BENEFIT OF THE DOUBT, DON'T DOUBT THE BENEFIT 129
- Building Trust 130
- **T**-R-U-S-T: Take the First Step 132
- T-**R**-U-S-T: Responsibility and Reliability 134
- T-R-**U**-S-T: Understanding 135
- T-R-U-**S**-T: Satisfying Needs 138
- T-R-U-S-**T**: Truthfulness Within 140

BE HONEST WITH YOURSELF AND OTHERS 144
- Authenticity 146
- Know Your Trends 147
- Know What Improvements You Need 148
- Live with Integrity 149
- Don't Assume Negatively 150
- Manage Your Emotions 151
- Truthfulness versus Authenticity 152

COMMUNICATE CLEARLY 159
- Confident Vulnerability 161
- Navigating Conflict 164
- Practice S-L-O-W 164
- Listen with Empathy 169

MAKE IT LAST 173
- A Quick Bolstering 175
- Sincerity 177
- Wrapping It Up 181

BONUS CHAPTER: IT'S ALL ABOUT RELATIONSHIPS 184

RESOURCES 198

Moving Beyond
Overthinking
in
Relationships

Preface

Tell me and I forget. Teach me and I remember. Involve me and I learn.
—Benjamin Franklin

My goal in writing this book is to allow the reader to learn about overthinking and its effect on relationships. A secondary goal is learning how to have better relationships in general. As a former teacher, I understand that students only learn when involved in the learning process. Reading can be passive if the reader is not encouraged to participate in the lessons within a book.

Therefore, as I pondered how to best present the material in this book, I considered incorporating review questions, exercises, and places to take notes within the text. But as I pondered, I realized that many people might not have a hardback or paperback copy of the book. Instead, many might have an eBook or audio version of the book. I realized that the readers needed something more to complete the learning process. My solution was to write a workbook, a separate book sold only in a paperback cover, as a companion to this book.

The workbook is titled *Moving Beyond Overthinking in Relationships Workbook.* It contains review, exercise, journaling, and note-taking sections. Each section allows the reader to become involved in the learning experience, making it more likely for them to learn the lessons in this book.

We will attempt to publish the workbook soon after this book becomes available, making it available to any who thinks they might benefit from it. I believe all readers will find it invaluable to understand how to get beyond overthinking and improve your relationships.

Whether you opt to use the workbook or not, I hope you'll benefit from the lessons I've learned over the years and find the help you are seeking.

a thinking society is a society that protects itself
from tyranny.

Thinking things through before making a decision is the only prudent way. Considering the ramifications of a decision is a core element of making wise decisions.

On the other hand, overthinking is a horse of a different color. It devolves into emotional thinking very quickly, and when a person falls into a habit of emotional thinking, that person overthinks. Emotions are tricky things. Thoughts full of good emotions make a person feel energized. However, if we make it a habit to have emotions as part of our thought processes, they have a nasty habit of devolving into negative emotions. Fear and doubt are the most common of these negative emotions. Fear and doubt combine to create the emotional state of anxiety.

A high school student might be very excited about an upcoming school play in which he or she has a significant role. As the event gets closer, the student starts thinking about the part he or she will play and how exhilarating it would feel to be on stage—in front of a whole lot of people. At that moment, doubt creeps in and they begin to have questions. What if I miss my cue and come in late? What if I forget my lines and just

Introduction
♦♦♦

Anxiety does not empty tomorrow o[f its sor]rows, but only empties today of its stre[ngth.]
—Charles Spurgeon

When I taught high school, I f[ound myself] constantly urging my students [to think, so] much so that one of my student[s made me] a little wooden placard that read, "THINK, [it's good for] all of us." I displayed the sign on my de[sk for many] years. I wanted my students to be able [to think for] themselves, and so I encouraged thoughtfu[l dialogue in] class.

Thinking, in and of itself, is an excell[ent thing to] do. A person who never learns to consider [a serious] matter but merely accepts every prop[osition that] sounds good is foolish. Many a tyrant ha[s used the] absence of thought as a means of power. I[n fact, the] stand there like a dork? What if people start to laugh? What if everybody knows me as *that person* who messed up the school play? How will I ever live that down? This sort of escalation of negative thoughts is called an overthinking cycle.

Most of us have probably experienced such a cycle in our lives. It may not be about a school play. It could be about anything that gives us a twinge of anxiety. Being anxious once in a while is a natural state of being. I don't know anyone who hasn't felt that prick of emotions at some point. It's the dwelling on anxiety that is at issue. It's incorporating that emotional state into our thinking that causes overthinking.

I have to assume that if you've read this far into this book about overthinking in relationships, you suspect that you've fallen prey to overthinking in a way that affects your relationships. I think it appropriate to see if overthinking is a problem for you. The following is a standard test commonly administered to know the extent of your problem. Please don't skip it. Understanding the degree of your overthinking issue will benefit you if you're serious about dealing with this potential problem.

On a separate sheet of paper or in the *Moving Beyond Overthinking in Relationships Workbook*, answer

the following questions honestly, using the following values:
- ❖ 1 for Never or almost never (I cannot recall doing this or not more than once or twice in my life)
- ❖ 2 for Rarely (it has happened a few times in my life)
- ❖ 3 for Sometimes (most days I don't)
- ❖ 4 for Often (more than you'd like)
- ❖ 5 for Constantly or nearly constantly (once or more nearly every day)

Once you've completed all twelve questions, add the number scores for all questions and write it at the top of your paper. You will find a key later in the book that will interpret your score.

A. Do you feel like your brain gets stuck in a loop, thinking about the same things repeatedly?

B. Do you find it sometimes difficult to make a decision because you get caught up in weighing the advantages and disadvantages?

C. Do you wonder if you've made the right decision after you've made it?

D. Do you find yourself regretting purchases you've made?

E. Do you find yourself worrying if you've forgotten to do something, like locking the door or turning off the stove?

F. Do you find your brain replays embarrassing experiences repeatedly for weeks, month or even years after the incident occurred?

G. Do you find yourself looking for negative connotations into harmless remarks that people make?
H. Do you replay conversations in your head or think about how you should have handled them differently after the fact?
I. Do you find yourself losing sleep because you're fixated on something you or someone else has said or done?
J. Do you feel that people frequently let you down or, conversely, that you're letting them down?
K. Do you negatively focus on the ambiguity of the words or actions of a friend, loved one, or significant other?
L. Do you find your mind wandering when everyone around you appears to be having a good time?

You may be wondering why the key is unavailable to you now. There are a couple of reasons. First, it's crucial for a person who overthinks, an overthinker, to see if impatience is a factor in their type of overthinking. If you feel that you can't live another moment without knowing, and the impulse to scour the book for the key right now is nearly overwhelming, then that answer is a resounding Yes! If you're feeling that strong impulse, deny yourself that impulse. Take a moment to take a deep breath, drink water or other non-alcoholic beverage, and relax for a few moments before reading more.

The second reason is to allow you to understand the consequences of overthinking before reviewing your assessment.

Overthinking can drastically affect many aspects of our lives, not just relationships. The key will reveal your degree of overthinking and, thus, how likely you are to fall under the influence of the consequences of overthinking.

Speaking of consequences, I'm reminded of a bout I had with overthinking. Not that long ago, I was in a job that I disliked. No, dislike is not a strong enough word; I HATED that job. It was a job I felt compelled to take because I found myself suddenly unemployed when the company I worked for decided to move out of the area. I was faced with having to choose between finding a job locally or moving over 700 miles to a more northern location. My family and I didn't want to move, so after looking for a couple of months for a job and getting the dreaded *overqualified* label on many of my applications, I settled on a job that met my financial needs. It wasn't long before I found that it didn't at all suit me at my stage in life.

That part of the cycle continued for a few months. Then, a new, more devastating cycle arose. My thoughts became darker. Here are some of them.

I can't quit, I have a family to support.

If I don't quit, I'm going to wear out my car and myself.

I can't quit, we'll lose the house.

If I don't quit, I'm going to end up in the hospital.

I can't quit. We'll all starve.

And so the thoughts grew more and more bleak. I was in decision paralysis. I was afraid to make any decision and forget trying to make the correct one.

Then, my dilemma grew. My wife, Jenny, developed a condition that made sleeping difficult. She could no longer work. My thoughts were already dark. These only deepened the hue of those illogical, emotional thoughts. It was a downward spiral that could have ended up in tragedy. But finally, I had a moment of clarity: a moment that eliminated my paralysis and gave me the answer to my predicament.

Let's discuss patience again. It's essential to learn. Patience can take the urgency from emotions and keep them from taking you on a rollercoaster ride that leads nowhere but back to where you started. I was impatient. That impatience is what trapped me in my

Introduction

The job involved a lot of travel in my personal vehicle; this put an unnatural strain on it. The job had irregular working hours. The job put enormous pressure on my family and me. On the job, I had to deal with many difficult people, putting tension in my emotions to the point where negative emotions entered my thinking.

After working the job for a few months, it dawned on me what it was doing to me and my family and friend relationships. It wasn't pretty. But instead of doing something about it, I thought about it—a lot!

My cycle went like this. My first thought was the only rational one: *I need to find a new job.* The second thought was a version of this: *I can't get another job in this field. Everyone will tell me I'm overqualified.* This was not a rational thought. Looking back, I hardly think that I had exhausted all possible employers during my previous job search.

The next thought went something like this: *Even there is a job for someone my age* (I was ancient for this particular field), *I don't have time to set up interviews.* There was some validation for that, considering the irregularity of my work hours, but I could take time off if necessary. So, this thought was invalid as well.

overthinking cycle. That's the point that I was driving toward.

I will finish my story later on in the book. If you're curious about it, that's okay; it means I did my job. On the other hand, if cutting off the story where I did drives you absolutely nuts, this is another opportunity to practice some patience. After all, if you can't conquer your impatience for the little things, how will you learn to beat it when bigger things come along?

Patience is not simply the ability to wait - it's how we behave while we're waiting.
—Joyce Meyer

Consider the following poem written by a person who was suffering from acute anxiety at the time of writing. She was able to put some of her thoughts into words.

Entangled
A Poem by Laura Farrell

I'm mourning the loss of you by myself
because you won't talk to me.
I'm mourning the loss of everyone I have lost
And everyone I will ever lose
in this same moment.

It started with you but then it expanded.
I'm mourning the loss of things,
Objects,
Ideas,
People that still exist but not to me.
I'm mourning the loss of what has been taken.
It all starts to compile into a list that runs through my head like
A news report,
"And on this day, hope was lost,"
So on
And so on
I've found hope again and again
through time and space
sometimes it takes a particular type of work,
that feels like digging
Right now it's buried somewhere I've forgotten,
like a time capsule with items from my childhood
but I cannot find my childhood home
and now I'm unsure if it ever existed.
Memory is funny because the more you return to it the further it becomes from the thing that actually happened.
It's like painting a picture without my glasses on,
This is what it is to recall.

Introduction

> Plus, I've never been a painter.
> Only language has allowed me to access things,
> and I speak in metaphor.
> Life is really some type of entanglement.
> I slow the news report down by drinking water,
> writing this poem,
> calling my mother.
> It's funny how things keep moving along anyway.
> I'm trying to keep count.
> I don't know what counts and what doesn't.
> I become lost in the meaning
> instead of the action.
> Instead of the feeling even.
> Sometimes I just need to figure out the reason.
> Most times there isn't any.

These eloquently worded thoughts give us a little insight into what deep anxiety can do to a human mind and the relationships surrounding that person. People in depression lose touch with those around them. No matter how insignificant, bad news adds to this hopeless feeling.

They can find hope, but it takes work, and hope is easily lost. Memories get distorted. Their mind becomes entangled. At the end, you see a thought cycle, ever searching for a reason to act. It is a snapshot of overthinking. Still, the poem shares more than my synopsis. It conveys emotion, for emotion colors everything for this person. In me, it stirs empathy. It helps me understand a little bit of what the writer is experiencing.

My encounter with overthinking is what prompted me to write this book. Here's what I hope you will gain from it.

First of all, I want you to grasp what overthinking is. The great Chinese General Sun Tzu once said, "Know thy self, know thy enemy. A thousand battles, a thousand victories." The enemy, in this case, is overthinking. What you don't know about it can hurt you. Forget preconceived notions when reading so that you can begin to understand what your enemy is out to do to you. To quote Socrates, "The only true wisdom is in knowing you know nothing."

Next, my goal is to teach simply. I don't want you bogged down in terminology, although I will use some. I'll focus more on giving a practical understanding of the lessons in the book. About science, Einstein said, "If you can't explain it simply, you don't understand it well enough."

The chapter headings encapsulate the lessons taught.

Introduction

View Overthinking as a Dilemma, not a Definition: Most people don't understand just how crippling overthinking can be. I hope to shed a bit of light on that. The key to the test you took earlier will also be in this chapter, just in case you need a little motivation to start the chapter.

Stop Trying to Read Smoke Signals: Overthinkers can get lost in interpreting what they see instead of stepping back and understanding that emotions might be coloring their interpretations. The lesson here is to see without the emotional filter.

Get off the Rumination Rollercoaster: I hope to give some practical methods to break the overthinking or rumination cycle in this chapter. I'll define triggers and provide a methodology for determining yours.

Give the Benefit of the Doubt, Don't Doubt the Benefit: This chapter is relationship-driven. Our state of mind always influences our reactions to others.

Be Honest with Yourself and Others: The merits of authenticity provide much of the content in this chapter. Learning to be honest with yourself is a lesson everyone still has to learn daily, but it is learnable. Once learned, it can help to stabilize you and, along with it, your relationships.

Make It Last: This is self-explanatory, really. This chapter contains some practical, timely advice on how to make your mindset and your relationship last.

Tips on How to Effectively Learn from this Book

I can be a voracious reader. As such, I've been known to devour a book this size in just a couple of hours. I don't recommend reading this book in such a manner. It is not a story of fiction that can be consumed plot point by plot point. Rather, consider it a book you must master to pass an exam created by a demanding teacher or professor. Only this time, the teacher is not a person; it is life itself—the ultimate in taskmasters.

Stop and meditate on any point that resonates with you. Those moments when you might say to yourself, "This guy is talking about me as if he can look inside my head." Not to worry, I'm not a psychic, nor do I play one on TV. I do have some insights on the subject of this book, however. Sometimes, I'll hit on something that hits home with you. When that happens, stop reading, take a moment, and write down whatever thought the reading portion gave you. Sure, you can underline parts of the book as well, but writing the precise thing the words on the page spoke to you is

Introduction

even more effective. Again, the workbook provides an effective way to take such notes.

As a teacher, I understand that people learn in many different ways, but one of the most important of those ways is reinforcement. Reinforcement for a young child might mean a repetitive drill, but in older children and adults, the best kind of reinforcement is the kind that is self-initiated. Writing down a related thought in your own words about what you just read is an excellent reinforcement tool.

Sometimes, exercises you can participate in alone or with your significant other are included in the book or the *Moving Beyond Overthinking in Relationships Workbook.* These are still different ways to reinforce and clarify what you glean in this book.

In other words, don't be in a hurry. Leave the rush outside and let yourself slow down. The popular expression says, "Give yourself some 'me' time." Take some time to reflect upon what you've read. As Confucius says, "By three methods we may learn wisdom: First, by reflection, which is noblest; Second, by imitation, which is easiest; and third by experience, which is the bitterest."

View Overthinking as a Dilemma, Not a Definition
❖◆❖

True happiness is...to enjoy the present, without anxious dependence upon the future.
—Lucius Annaeus Seneca

The ancient Roman philosopher Seneca attempted to define happiness in the quote above. Admittedly, it's not a complete definition, but it has truth connected to it. Enjoying life without anxiousness gives us reason to identify that enjoyment as happiness. Of course, happiness is fleeting in life simply because enjoyment is not a permanent state. No one can describe themselves as happy whose present circumstances are not enjoyable. But enjoying something in life is not the same as having joy. Can you have joy by simply not worrying about the future? No. But the absence of worry does make it possible to enjoy the parts of life that one considers enjoyable. Constant worry about the future robs an individual of enjoyment of even the most enjoyable activities.

If we take Seneca's statement as a valid statement, and if we know that overthinking feeds on doubt and fear, the source of anxiousness, it can be deduced that overthinking, therefore, robs a person of enjoyment and, thus, happiness. Further, it follows that if we are deprived of happiness, it is logical to assume that the lack of happiness in our lives would adversely affect the lives of those with whom we have relationships. This line of reasoning thus concludes that overthinking is a problem in a relationship, but if you're an overthinker, you are probably already aware of that; else, why the interest in this book? But are there other less obvious consequences to overthinking?

A Definition of Overthinking

The Merriam-Webster Dictionary defines overthinking this way: "to think too much about (something) : to put too much time into thinking about or analyzing (something) in a way that is more harmful than helpful."

From the definition alone, we can spot another problem with overthinking. It wastes time. The time spent is causing more harm than good; therefore, it is wasted time. But what are the damages? I'm sure the definition has more in mind than only relationships, or it would have specified relationship as the harm, would it not?

Since we've established that overthinking harms relationships, wastes time, and has harmful effects outside of relationships, now is an excellent time to give you the scoring key of the overthinking test you took back in the introduction to the book. Perhaps the results will provide you with more pause about your tendency to overthink than it would have before you became aware of the possibility of more harmful consequences. The key is on the next page.

Total Score	Indication
12-17	You have the lowest tendency possible toward overthinking.
18-29	You have a slight tendency toward overthinking.
30-38	You have a moderate tendency toward overthinking. Under stressful conditions, you will tend to overthink.
39-48	You have a high tendency toward overthinking. Relationships are likely to be affected. You may have a tendency to overthink decisions, especially ones you consider more important. There is a possibility of Decision Paralysis in such cases.
49-60	You have severe tendencies toward overthinking. Relationships will be a problem eventually, if they are not already being affected. You are very likely to develop Decision Paralysis even with minor decisions.

As a reference, I scored as a slight to moderate risk for overthinking when administered the test in a study at work a few months before that company moved out of town. I dismissed it thinking, I guess I'm alright since I wasn't a high or severe risk. The truth is we don't know how we'll react under pressure until we react. Any risk level should admonish us to be vigilant in monitoring our thinking habits.

Something to Think About

How did you handle delayed gratification by waiting to present this key until now? Did it initially make you annoyed in any way? Were you tempted to flip through the book until you found the key? Did you put aside any urges or feelings and wait until you came across the key in the ordinary course of reading? If you can answer yes to that last question, despite responding yes to one or more of the previous questions, you have taken a little step toward patience.

If any person had the opportunity to be impatient, it was Helen Keller. She was born deaf and blind. If you're unfamiliar with her story, it's worth studying. She was able to make her life a testimony of patience. Here is what she had to say when asked about her challenges: "We could never learn to be brave and patient, if there were only joy in the world."

Learn to be patient in the little things first; when the more significant challenges come along, the patience you've learned will be able to handle them.

Detrimental Mental Transition

To review what we discussed in the introduction, the two prominent emotions that trigger overthinking are fear and doubt. Anxiety manifests fear and doubt, which the body responds to in stress. Throwing another term into the mix, anxiety is often referenced as worry, although they are not entirely synonymous. Anxiety is technically a mental reaction to worry, tenseness, or fear. Still, I find that most folks identify with the term worry better than anxiety. For our discussion, let's think of worry as a condition that plagues the mind and stress as a condition that afflicts the body.

So, if you start to feel fear or doubt, your mind starts to worry. Worrying leads to more chronic conditions of the mind. One of these is Generalized Anxiety Disorder, or GAD for short. GAD means having regular, sometimes uncontrolled worries about any number of things. One way in which GAD manifests itself is overthinking.

Unchecked overthinking results in a series of overthinking cycles that, in turn, result in repetitive thinking that can become repetitive urges, which, in turn, can trigger repetitive behaviors. This condition is called Obsessive-Compulsive Disorder, more commonly known as OCD. This path is one of many detrimental directions that your mind can take with fear and doubt.

FEAR and DOUBT → GAD → Overthinking → Repetitive Behavior → OCD
Typical Mental Transition to OCD

This progression is certainly not the only detrimental path the mind can take from fear and doubt, but it is one where overthinking plays a substantial role. Tuck this away somewhere if you ever feel inclined to take overthinking lightly. It is certainly not meant to give you more ammunition for your overthinking.

Stress on Your Body and Behavior

Stress, worry, and overthinking feed off of each other. Overthinking produces more worry. Worry, in turn, puts stress on our bodies. Stress can affect your health, even though you might not realize it. Stress can cause irritating headaches and frequent insomnia, decreasing productivity in our daily routine. But it doesn't stop there.

The body has many ways to indicate that it is stressed. Overall, muscle tension and pain are linked with stress. Even your heart is not immune to this effect, adding the symptom of chest pain to the list. Because of the muscle tension, fatigue can set in, making you feel tired even if you've rested a good portion of the day. This tension can even spill over to your digestive system, making things go wonky with your stomach and intestines.

Because of the tension and disorder in your body, your mind produces more worry. In turn, this affects our behavior. The extra focus our mind puts on our body maladies affects our ability to focus on things around us. The distraction in our minds makes us less motivated to do what we planned or promised, leading to procrastination. We can become restless, wanting to do something but unable to focus enough to decide. Your mind tells you, "I'm not in the mood to do anything." In contrast, because of the hyperactivity of your mind, you can experience a feeling of being overwhelmed.

The reduced production creates an argument within yourself. "Get this done," you tell yourself. Your mind responds, "Maybe later." You will try to take over. "I am going to do this." But your mind ignores your will. This argument spills outward in irritability and anger, alienating those around you. Finally, sadness floods your mind. You feel worthless and angry with yourself, ultimately leading to depression.

Our bodies and our minds are interlinked like that. Overthinking is the first step in fueling negative emotions and triggering the body to respond in kind. It all can become a vicious cycle.

> *A healthy outside starts from the inside."*
> —Robert Urich

Traumatic Events and Perfectionism

Most everyone has been through a stressful event in his or her life. When the event, or series of events, causes a lot of stress, it is called a traumatic event. A sense of horror, helplessness, serious injury, or the threat of severe injury or death marks traumatic events. Here's the tricky part: threats caused by an event can be genuine or merely perceived as reality. If your mind perceives extreme peril, even if there is no real peril, your mind will treat that event as traumatic.

Whatever the case, real or perceived, these events leave indelible markers on our minds. A person struck by a car on a street will react differently to the sound of an approaching car than someone who hasn't experienced that trauma. In the same way, a person whose mind convinces them that they were nearly run down by a car, even if that was not the reality of the situation, may exhibit the same type of reaction to an approaching car as the person who was actually struck.

One of my co-workers at a past job absolutely refused to walk anywhere near a busy street. Why? Because of an incident in her childhood while walking near a busy street. That's the way she described it. When others inquired about the event, she never gave specifics; she never admitted to being hit or almost hit by a car, nor would she say another person was struck. She wouldn't even say a vehicle hit a pet or her pet had a near miss. To this day, I don't know why she had this aversion to walking near a busy street. It could be that it had nothing to do with the street itself, but somehow, walking near a busy street triggers something that happened near a busy street that made her feel in danger. Only one thing is sure: her mind has convinced her that walking near a busy street is unsafe.

You might be thinking that her fear is irrational. Well, of course, it is. But rational thinking was not the cause of this aversion; it was developed through emotional thinking, overthinking in other words. Reasonable or not, the fear is now real to that woman. Perhaps she was in real danger at that time in the past; maybe she was not. It matters not, for the fear is still tangible in her mind, all through the power of overthinking.

Admittedly, that example was a bit incomplete because I could never learn everything surrounding it. So here is another example where all the facts are known. A fellow principal at a teacher's conference related this story to me.

A valedictorian adamantly refused to give a speech at graduation. In fact, the student was shaking and practically in tears. The faculty was baffled. The student had excelled at public speaking during high school. The student had performed brilliantly just a month before, having a starring role in the school play.

The principal approached the parents of the student to see if there was a reason that they didn't want the student to speak. Turned out, the parents were just as baffled as the staff.

Finally, a fellow student who was a close friend managed to get an answer to the perplexing refusal. The valedictorian of the class had convinced himself that everyone in the school was either angry or laughing at him. The only evidence he gave to his friend was his awful performance during the school play.

The principal was more confused than ever. He remembered a stellar performance by the future valedictorian. The play had been videotaped, so the principal reviewed the tape with the play's director. As he had remembered, the performance by the distressed student was sensational. But both the director and the principal noticed an anguished look on the student's face near the end of the last scene that didn't fade as the curtain closed.

At the curtain call, the valedictorian did not appear. The director recalled that the student had said he felt sick. The director hadn't given it much thought, and it wasn't noticeable on tape that there was any particular notice of the missing actor by the cast or audience.

Then, the director rewound the tape to the last scene and watched it carefully. He shrugged his shoulders and told the principal that the only thing he noticed was that the character played by the valedictorian omitted a minor line. The principal asked the director to point out the missed line to him. Sure enough, it was right after the missed line that the sour expression appeared on the troubled student's face.

That one missed line was the cause of all the angst. "You see," the principal told me, "that student was a perfectionist."

Perfectionism is another root cause of overthinking. What caused the student to believe that his performance in the school play made everyone angry or, if they were not, had turned the whole school into mockers?

Here's my theory of a possible path of progression.
1. The student realized he missed the line only after it was too late to say it.
2. The student became visibly distraught nearly right away.
3. The student dwelt on the mistake making himself physically ill. He probably wasn't lying when he had said that he was ill after the play.
4. Because he was absent during curtain call and no one seemed to miss him, his pride was hurt.
5. The hurt pride along with dwelling on his mistake triggered the start of an overthinking cycle.
6. The cycle grew within his mind, becoming ever more dominant and dark.
7. At some point he came to the conclusion that he had ruined the play.
8. That thought elevated the play to being the biggest disaster in school history.
9. That thought give rise to the thought that everyone hated him.
10. The natural end of being hated was for his naysayers to mock him.

I cannot be sure if the sequence of thought followed that exact pattern; it may have had a few more twists and turns since the young man was brilliant. That intellect could have concocted a very convoluted path to the end of his journey. Nevertheless, the mind journey was taken, and the damage to his psyche will stick with him for a while.

Why did I link so closely together a story about trauma and a story about perfectionism? They are both paths to a similar end. The woman's trauma might have resulted from a real threat, or maybe not. Regardless, the woman still feels the threat, imagined or not. The trauma that perfectionism brought the student was primarily a perceived trauma. The only real difference is that we know that the perfectionist made a mountain out of a molehill, but the woman might have experienced a real threat or shock to her psyche. They are still very much related to each other—the lasting effects of trauma, whether self-induced or not, are unmistakable.

The start of the overthinking cycle that I recounted in the introduction started with a traumatic event for me. It was the first time in my life that I had ever had an unsuccessful interview for a job. The fact that it wasn't only one but multiple rejections impacted me. The reason given for the refusal was baffling to me. I thought, "If I exceed the qualifications, want the job, and am happy with the salary, why shouldn't I have been hired?" That thought led to the belief that no one would hire me in that field no matter what, and it's the thought that stuck with me throughout my overthinking cycle. Now, was my trauma real or only perceived? I'll leave you with that thought.

Time for a Little Levity

Since the last few pages were getting pretty serious, let's lighten things up with a little overthinking humor.

> An overthinker's boss is two minutes late for a one-on-one meeting.
> ***Overthinker:*** *"Were we really supposed to meet at this time? Is this the right conference room? Is it actually Thursday today? Were we even meeting on Thursday? Do I actually know that we were supposed to meet? Do I still have a job? Does my boss actually exist? Do I exist?"*

Sometimes, making light can change our perspective a bit. It never hurts to poke a little fun at yourself as long as it doesn't turn negative. The over-exaggeration of the progression here is funny, but it also illustrates how easily overthinking can progress to exaggerated levels.

The Science behind Overthinking

There are two schools of thought on the relationship between the mind and the brain. Some scientists hold that the brain produces the mind. That is why when the brain malfunctions, the mind malfunctions. When the brain dies, the mind dies. This view comes from the idea that matter and energy are the only real things in the universe. The data used to back this up concerns the firing of synapsis in different brain regions. For example, when asleep, the unconscious mind is active. The cortex is dormant during this time, and the activity is centered in the basal ganglia and cerebellum. When awake, the conscious mind takes over, and the main activity in the brain moves to the cortex because the cortex is again producing the conscious mind.

Scientists majoring in the field of psychology hold to another school of thought. This view allows that the mind is separate from the brain and controls the parts of the brain that seem to produce thought. When a brain is injured, the mind is wounded only because it cannot utilize the part of the damaged brain. Eventually, the mind will find another part of the brain to use. Patients who've suffered significant injury to the brain and still regained full or nearly complete cognitive abilities support this view. By the same logic, this view theorizes that the cortex shutting down to rest induces sleep, so the mind goes into its standby mode, the unconscious state, and finds different areas of the brain to operate during this time. Both of these views are oversimplified here for brevity's sake.

You may lean toward one or the other, but I agree with the second view because it better explains the elephant in the room: the subconscious mind. The subconscious mind is estimated to cause up to 95% of the brain activity during waking hours. We are unaware of the subconscious mind but can't function well without it. It is a ready access for memory, the simple facts, like your telephone number. Your mind flashes to the information when someone asks for your telephone number. Before the question, it most likely was not part of your conscious thought, but after you heard the question, now it is. Unless you've forgotten it, meaning you either never committed it to memory, or it has been too long since you did so, and other thoughts have buried the information. This happenstance is an indication of the limitations that our mind has because of its current dependence on the brain. Eventually, if you focus on it long enough, the number will most likely come to you if it's in your mind somewhere.

The subconscious mind is a bustling place. It's where our behaviors, habits, moods, beliefs, values, and interpretation of our physical senses are stored. Our subconscious allows us to see a bird and know what it is, to hear a sound and know where it came from, to identify a familiar smell, to recognize a typical taste, and to feel comforted by a loved one's touch.

Our subconscious minds also tell us when something is wrong in our body and give it meaning beyond the mere signals our brain receives. And it is our subconscious that responds to our brain chemistry.

There are four hormones that our bodies secrete that have an immediate impact on our subconscious minds. Most of us are familiar with adrenaline. It is the hormone that makes our heart beat faster. It's a powerful stimulant. Less familiar might be dopamine. Dopamine is sometimes called the satisfaction hormone or the reward hormone. It's released when we feel a sense of accomplishment, for example. Serotonin is a mood regulator, sometimes called the feel-good hormone. And cortisol is the stress hormone. It increases tension not only in our muscles but also in our minds.

These four hormones play a significant role in overthinking. Even though overthinking devolves into a riot of negative emotions, it doesn't start that way. It begins with a problem-solving task initiated by the subconscious. This action causes the mind to call for dopamine to assist and encourage the task in our conscious mind. Because problem-solving significantly increases brain activity, the subconscious calls for adrenaline to give our brain energy for the task. Excitement also builds in our minds at this time. As new options emerge, there is a call for serotonin. Serotonin makes us feel good and encourages our minds to continue. If the problem-solving sequence doesn't produce satisfactory results, our negative mood within our subconscious summons cortisol and stress is the result. The stress in our mind makes us question if it's worth it, but in the overthinker, the mind craves more dopamine and serotonin, so the mind loop continues. Now comes the invasion of negative emotions of whatever sort is appropriate for the frustration that the mind is experiencing. Thinking about this problem becomes an addiction. Your subconscious mind refuses to quit. Eventually, our conscious mind becomes aware of the negativity and shuts down the cycle. Yet, when overthinking becomes chronic, the subconscious will initiate the process again, and on and on, the subconscious goes.

So, in a way, overthinking is a faulty subconscious mind. Something is just not right with our behavioral mechanisms. Or perhaps the problem lies with our habits. Maybe the problem lies with our belief system. Or, just perhaps, it has something to do with our core values. Whatever the case, the subconscious mind is not easily changed.

Therein lies the dilemma. The problem doesn't go away independently; thinking about it only makes you feel worse. However, you become trapped in having to think about it just one more time. But that one more time turns into another, then another, and then it morphs into endless cycles of "just one more time."

Overthinking's Effect on Relationships

> *Anxiety is love's greatest killer. It makes others feel as you might when a drowning man holds on to you. You want to save him, but you know he will strangle you with his panic.*
> —Anais Nin

Anais Nin wrote about the infatuation of love quite a bit. I think it significant that she recognizes the power of anxiety over even love's passion. With that sort of power, what chance do other types of relationships have against it? The anxiety upon which overthinking feeds does not just affect the person with the anxiety; it also affects those closest to that person.

Let's take in a scenario. You're an overthinker. You see your close friend walking across from you on a busy street. You shout hello to your friend and wave. Your friend looks in your direction, but instead of returning the greeting, your friend just keeps walking as if you never said anything. You think, "I know they saw me, but they just ignored me. Did I do something to upset them? Am I no longer someone they want to know? Am I not good enough for them?" This questioning goes on for a while in your mind until you become pretty upset. The next time you see your friend, it's a similar chance meeting on the street. This time, your friend greets you. But you're still seething inside and not thinking clearly. You don't respond to your friend but stare angrily in your friend's direction for a few seconds before continuing on your way. What do you think the friend in this scenario might be thinking?

Here's another scenario, this time with a significant other. You're an overthinker. You just had a doctor's appointment today and made your spouse aware of it.

View Overthinking as a Dilemma, Not a Definition

It was a routine visit, and nothing out of the ordinary occurred. Later that evening, your spouse came home looking exhausted. You exchanged pleasantries and had supper together and talked of trivial matters. But your spouse failed to ask you about your appointment during that time. You think, "How selfish and insensitive! He (she) doesn't care about me. I'm alone in this relationship." You believe such thoughts most of the evening. It comes time to go to bed. Your spouse is going to bed and comes to give you a good night's kiss. Instead of kissing on the lips, you turn your cheek to your spouse. After you receive a peck on the cheek, you ask, "Why don't you care for me like you used to?" How will your spouse react?

In both scenarios, overthinking invented a worst-case scenario out of what could have been utterly innocent behavior. The overthinker failed to consider all the alternatives. Your friend could have heard something and turned to see what it was but didn't see you across the street. Your spouse could have had a trying day and other things to think about that evening. Overthinkers tend to believe they're communicating in their relationships, but in reality, communication is one way. Most communications with others are about themselves, and they come off as being needy or clingy. They interpret rather than see, as in the first example. They tend to lack empathy for others, as in the second example. The overthinker didn't consider the exhaustion that his or her spouse exhibited. Overthinking makes maintaining relationships stressful for both parties and is intensified in close relationships.

Relationship overthinking (or, as some call it, rumination) comes in at least five forms, each one having a slightly different motivation.

The Blame Game Cycle

The blame game is motivated by a need for blame to be assigned. Either you or the other person is at fault. You recall the past selectively to prove you or the other person is to blame. Initial thoughts center on blame. *This is my fault. I'm such an idiot. How could I let this happen?* Or conversely, *They should pay for this. They should apologize. Don't they realize how much pain they're causing me?*

The Self-pity Cycle

Frequently, the subconscious expectation is that by clinging to the role of a victim, you'll inspire your rela-

View Overthinking as a Dilemma, Not a Definition

tionship partner to rescue you. But they feel controlled when you make your partner the responsible party for your well-being or behave as though you're entirely helpless when you're not. This cycle initiates with these types of thoughts: *Why me? There's nothing I can do. Life is unfair. I don't deserve this. Why is it always me?*

The Worry Cycle

In this cycle, worst-case scenarios rule. Fear keeps this cycle going. Your subconscious goes immediately to thinking how everything could go wrong. The initial thoughts include: *What if they stop loving me? She might cancel our next date if she finds out I'm an overthinker. One of us could get sick and make the elderly father seriously ill. I'm happy right now, but it won't last.*

The Control Freak Cycle

Thoughts tend to have a dogmatic edge and include ultimatums. You believe in externally defined truths and are the only one who knows what they are. Here are some possible initial thoughts: *I know best. My views should hold sway. They must quit [fill in be-*

havior], or I'm done. It's time to talk about [fill in the perceived problem], or I won't fulfill [fill in some relationship need].

The Doubt Trip Cycle

In this cycle, there's never enough certainty. No evidence is ever powerful enough to support your choices, decisions, or actions. Self-doubt and insecurity are the banner traits in this cycle. Initial thoughts may include: *Did this actually happen, or is it just me? Why is every other couple doing better than we are? Why did I choose my partner? Why did my partner choose me? Am I a fraud? Can I trust my own choices?*

Some of these cycle labels may overlap in some people. It's not uncommon for an overthinker to have multiple triggering thoughts from different cycle types. But the point is, none of these sorts of deliberations would be able to start a relationship, but each one is very capable of ending one.

A Faith-Based Perspective on Overthinking

Perspectives are interesting things. If you're familiar with sports broadcasts, whether on TV or radio, there are typically two broadcasters calling a game.

View Overthinking as a Dilemma, Not a Definition

One is the play-by-play broadcaster. His job is to let people know what is happening in the game. In football, he'll relate who carried, threw, or caught the ball and how much yardage was gained. He may tell who made the tackle if a tackle was made on the play. He describes the play's direction on the field, *handoff up the middle,* or *pass to the right flat,* that sort of detail. He may comment on the nature of the play in some way: *What a fantastic catch!* But that's pretty much his function. The other broadcaster is the commentator. It's a commentator's job to bring more detail to the game. He tells you why a particular play worked or didn't work. He gives you details about preparation by a player or coach. He'll even provide a short anecdote about someone involved or associated with the game. Or if the game is a blowout, he might even break out a story about a game in the past or something that happened to him that day, anything to keep people tuned into the game. The subconscious mind is the commentator for our lives. It is there that life gains meaning and purpose. It's all about the perspective that your commentator, your subconscious, provides.

Perspectives are shaped by what we experience in life. Don't think that this only happens in our childhood; our views are being shaped every day by our decisions, by our relationships, by what we experience, and by what knowledge we gain. Unless we close off our minds to an "I only believe what I believe" mentality, we can grow our perspective.

However, I'm not considering growing our perspectives by accepting any idea or thought that comes along. That would be disastrous. It is to this fallacy that the overthinker falls victim. The rumination of thought mixed with his worries, care, and anxiety produce false facts; some call them pseudo-facts. To base our perspectives on such "facts" is likened to building a house on the sand in Scripture.

It is popular to have your own truth today. I see slogans urging people to find their own truth. This mantra is confusing. What does that mean?

Is truth something that changes depending on philosophy or disposition? Does it change because the other truth makes me uncomfortable? Does it vary by the will of the mind? If that were the case, overthinking would be the healthiest practice in the world. All truth would bend to your choice. That sounds like paradise to an overthinker. Or is it? Overthinking is a problem because the "house" they build is like the house built on the sand. It is susceptible to any movement the

View Overthinking as a Dilemma, Not a Definition

sand might make. Have you ever been in a sandstorm? If you have, you know that sand can move quite a bit.

This idea that truth is malleable isn't prevalent only today. This idea of shifting truth was commonplace in the ancient Roman Empire. When Christ stood before Pilate in the judgment hall, Pilate asked Him, "Are you a king then?" Jesus answered, "Thou sayest that I am a king. To this end was I born, and for this cause came I into the world, that I should bear witness unto the truth. Every one that is of the truth heareth my voice." Notice the use of the word *truth* in Jesus's answer. Jesus used it twice, and both times, it was preceded by the definite article, *the.* It wasn't any truth; it was *the truth* that Jesus referenced. Pilate replied, "What is truth?" Then he left the judgment hall as if to say that's all there is to discuss. Yet he could have discussed what truth was. Instead, he merely expressed an opinion about the philosophy prevalent in his day that everyone could have their own personal truth. He saw all the "truths" and felt compelled to ask, probably sardonically, "What is truth?" This philosophy was what fueled the gnostic sect of the early church. But I digress.

Does "the truth" exist? Well, Jesus believed it did.

C. S. Lewis wrote: "If you look for truth, you may find comfort in the end; if you look for comfort you will not get either comfort or truth only soft soap and wishful thinking to begin, and in the end, despair."

People who seek only comfort in life end up in despair. The thinking goes something like this: Truth is not the issue; it's what makes life comfortable that matters. To phrase it another way, what I concoct in my mind is what matters. Doesn't that sound like the overthinking dilemma?

Scripture speaks about overthinking. The word *overthinking* doesn't appear since this word is a relatively recent concoction in English. But the word *careful* is used. At the time of the Scripture's translation into English, the word *careful* had two dominant meanings. The first was "full of care," today we might say, "full of worry." The second is the word's primary meaning today for most people: "to be attentive or watchful."

Using the first definition of careful read Philippians 4:6: "Be careful for nothing; but in every thing by prayer and supplication with thanksgiving let your requests be made known unto God."

What word would we use today to mean "full of care"? It's *anxious*. What is the cause of overthinking?

View Overthinking as a Dilemma, Not a Definition

Well, that would be anxiousness in its various forms. Scripture tells us to be not to be that way. Don't be an overthinker! Then, it gives some advice for the person who has faith. Pray about everything and ask God when you have need (supplications) with thanksgiving. Prayer is really about meditation and communication. Think about God and the truth that God has given us, and then talk to Him in faith and trust. Nearly every psychologist recommends meditation as part of a recovery therapy for overthinking. The faith version of meditation involves prayer. At the risk of giving away another topic later in the book, did you know that a recent German study showed that gratitude (another word for *thankfulness* or *thanksgiving*) plays a significant role in stress reduction? Psychologists now view thanksgiving as a tool to help overcome many anxiety conditions, including overthinking. I had to chuckle when I read multiple sources that described gratitude as a "new way to deal with anxiousness." I guess it's new if you consider an at least two-thousand-year-old concept as being new. It's a shame that such an excellent resource for relationship council is just gathering dust on many shelves today. Scripture has a wealth of counseling on many things, but you could say that human and divine relationship counseling is a specialty of Scripture.

A Personal Note from the Author

I am not a perfect person. You already know that because I've already admitted to being caught up in overthinking earlier in my life. Well, I'm about to double down on my imperfection by telling you the following story. But I trust that this story will be of benefit.

You already know that I was not in a good place mentally when I was doing that hated job. As you may recall, that job required me to travel quite a bit on appointments. According to Google Maps, I was driving to an appointment 30 miles away. It was 10:25, and the meeting was for 11:00. I was traveling in South Carolina on a winding road that did not afford the ability to pass another vehicle. According to my route, I was to be on this road for 25 miles before taking a major highway the rest of the way to my appointment. The speed limit was 40 mph on this road. I did the rudimentary math in my head and knew that it would take me more time to get to the major route than I had to get to my appointment.

View Overthinking as a Dilemma, Not a Definition

Now, there wasn't any significant consequence to being a few minutes late to these appointments because of the unpredictable time element inherent in my work. But my mind had conjured up terrible consequences for being late due to an abundance of emotional thinking I had going on at the time. So, I quickly deduced that if I went 50 mph for the duration of the road, I would just about be able to make my appointment on time.

So there I was, tooling down this winding road at 50 mph. With about 15 miles left on the road, I saw a car just disappearing out of sight on the curve ahead. I didn't know if the vehicle had just turned onto the road or if I was catching up to it. I hoped it was the former.

After finishing the next curve, I had my answer. The car in front of me appeared on the road, much closer to me than before. I sighed, coasted up closer to the car, and matched the car's speed. The vehicle was going almost precisely 40 mph.

So, being the person I was then, what did I do? I got angry. After all, who was this insolent driver up ahead who dared to make me late for my appointment? I briefly thought about trying to pass the driver despite the double yellow line on the pavement, but then a large cargo truck came around the bend, putting self-preservation to the forefront of my mind. So, I reluctantly fell back slightly and followed the car at a respectful distance. But all the while I was on that road, I had terrible thoughts about the driver of that car, imagining them to be selfish for daring to get in my way. If it wasn't the label of selfishness, I was applying the label of arrogance. Who do they think they are? Then I tried on a few other labels, none flattering to the driver or me, for that matter.

In retrospect, I now realize that the driver's motivation was likely not malignant. The rationale behind that driver's adherence to the speed limit was probably simply to do the right thing.

This story illustrates a prevalent view of the Christian faith: Christianity is a restrictive religion. Most folks in our society value personal freedom. A standard definition for many is the freedom to choose your own life path and be yourself. In this view, Christianity is like living life in a straitjacket.

However, this is the view of someone driving behind that law-abiding driver. What if you were traveling with that driver? You're a passenger in the car, and you're progressing down the road at a legal pace. The driver is not anxious but relaxed. The driver's state of mind and control of the vehicle also lets you relax. Looking out the window, you see the beauty of the hills. You see wildlife in the distance, and you find yourself immersed in the scenes that flow by outside the car.

Now you hear honking from behind the car, interrupting your serenity. You turn to see a vehicle tailgating your car. You shake your head and wonder what's eating that driver. You find empathy for that driver and his passengers. You wish that you could share some of the serenity with those in the car behind you.

That's my motivation for using a touch of scripture within this discourse. I merely want to share some of my serenity with you. If you're open to exploring more of that serenity, there is a bonus chapter at the end of the book that plumbs more of the depth of the wisdom of scripture concerning relationships. I trust it will benefit you as much as it has helped me.

Stop Trying to Read Smoke Signals
◆❖◆

Most of us are probably familiar with smoke signals from movies about the Old West. Perhaps you thought smoke signals were just an invention of Hollywood. In reality, smoke signals are a real thing. The North American native tribes used bonfires for transmitting messages, even complex ones. Hollywood even got the method of making them correct. By covering the fire with a blanket or hide and exposing it for measured periods, they created small smoke clouds that they could mold into varying shapes. The number of clouds, shape of the clouds, and interval between them could all have a specific meaning.

The most simple and universal signals that many tribes used were the one, two, or three puffs of smoke.

One puff meant to pay attention, something is going on here; two puffs meant all is well; and three puffs meant danger or help. Yet, the messages were often encoded so that only the sender and receiver could interpret them correctly. This coding allowed them to convey messages privately, even though the smoke was visible to all in the region.

It was the quickest way to communicate with others over a distance that the natives had. However, the more intricate the signal was, the more difficult it was to send. It took skill to make some of the shapes necessary. If they sent a wrong shape, there was little to do to take it back. It was already there for all to see. If a strong breeze arose, it could alter shapes and make the message unreadable or misunderstood.

In short, smoke signals, although clever, weren't a highly efficient way to communicate. It took a while to formulate a message, and there was too much chance of ambiguity.

Regularly, overthinking sees messages in actions, non-actions, and expressions of others that can lead to ambiguity of thought and false translations of the motives of others. Impatience plays a role in this method of "fact accumulation." An overthinker will use this method when other forms of communication are not immediately available, even if the lack of different forms of communication is not the fault of the other person in question. Fear of confrontation concerning a perceived slight, a question of fidelity, or dread of knowing how another person feels about some aspect of the relationship can cause the overthinker to delay communication. Thus, they resort to the smoke signals method to communicate from a distance despite the possibility of ambiguity and misinterpretation.

Here's a little humor to illustrate the point.

> An Indian Chief was taking a week off in Las Vegas. After just two days, he had gambled away all his funds, so he sent a smoke signal back to his tribe asking them to wire him more money.
>
> The tribe signaled back, saying "No way, you're being reckless with your money and we're not sending you any more!"
>
> Just then, a nuclear bomb was detonated in the Nevada desert. The Chief watched in awe as the gigantic mushroom cloud reached toward the sky.
>
> Then, further in the distance, he saw a tiny plume of smoke that said "OK, we'll send you more money! No need to scream like that!"

Stop Trying to Read Smoke Signals

Like the tribe in this humorous story, the overthinker interprets signals that may not even be from the relationship partner. They could be signals from a friend of a friend. They could be from a spouse's relative. They could even be from a child of the family whose actions or out-of-context words convey smoke signals about the other person in the relationship. The reasons for this extra-partnership signal reading tend to get somewhat convoluted in the overthinking mind.

So, what can be done about this propensity to read smoke signals? The first thing is that you have to believe that you *can* change. Then you have to *want* to change. If you cannot get to that place, no method, technique, or steps in this world will work for you.

One of the biggest problems people have is admitting they have a problem. They say things like, "It's just the way, I am," or my personal favorite, "that's the way God made me," to validate themselves. The truth is that God didn't make anyone robotic or static. He gave them the capacity to change, but we must want to change.

The Pharisees were a sect of the Jewish religion that emphasized the "traditions of the fathers" over the Scripture available in that day. They allied themselves in opposition to Jesus in his ministry and were the chief instrument in his eventual crucifixion. They taught adherence to some burdensome practices, but Jesus observed that they did not follow them. Jesus ultimately pronounced the famous woes on them in the book of Matthew. After Jesus pronounced woe on the Pharisees and other leaders of the Jews, He lamented over Jerusalem, saying, "O Jerusalem, Jerusalem, thou that killest the prophets, and stonest them which are sent unto thee, how often would I have gathered thy children together, even as a hen gathereth her chickens under her wings, and ye would not!" Why did they not respond to Jesus's repeated calls to change their ways? Because they *couldn't*? No, that wasn't the problem. Please take a look at it again. It's because they *would not*. Why do some folks never change? It's because they *will not*, not because they *cannot*. They simply *will* not take action necessary to change.

Why is that? For many, it's a problem that John Ruskin noted saying, "In general, pride is at the bottom of all great mistakes." Why was the mistake so great? Pride either fueled it or got in the way of correcting it.

For others, it's fear. The fear of doing is something the overthinking mind has in abundance. Here's a scenario to consider.

An overthinker is knocked out and put into a deep pit without food or water. The pit has three possible means of escape: a rickety ladder, a worn rope, and a crumbling rocky slope. The overthinker may ruminate endlessly about which of the escape options is the least dangerous. Fear may paralyze the overthinker. Will the overthinker take a chance for life by taking action or stay helplessly at the bottom, looking up in despair, crying for help that will never come?

That's the mental dilemma some of you may be facing now.

A well-known radio personality, Dave Ramsey, who had overcome many personal issues, said, "Hitting bottom and hitting it hard was the worst thing that ever happened to me and the best thing that ever happened to me." Why? Because the hard hits of life made him finally take action. How far into the depths of overthinking will you have to go to decide to take action ultimately? Will you remain stuck in that pit with your fixed mindset, or will you adopt a growth mindset that compels you to take action? The choice is yours.

Curiosity

Up to now, I've focused on the problem of overthinking. It's time to shift gears and get into some ways to move beyond overthinking, especially in relationships.

So we've decided that we want to grow and change. How can we keep that mindset? One of the easiest ways is to stay curious.

James Stephens was best known for his role as James T. Hart in the television series *The Paper Chase,* popular in the late '70s and early '80s. He endured his share of setbacks as a struggling actor in the early '70s. When he finally had success, he said when asked what kept him going during the lean years, "Curiosity will conquer fear even more than bravery will." Curiosity in this context is a willingness to learn. Stephens's desire to grow as an actor conquered his fear of rejection.

Be willing to admit what you don't know and follow that up with the curiosity to understand your relationship issues better. How are internalized experiences affecting your relationships? How are your vulnerabilities influencing your interactions? Be curious to discover things about the people in your relationships. What drives them and makes them happy? Curiosity should not be a means to an end, forgotten when you resolve one relationship curiosity. It should be an end in itself, a never-ending quest to learn, motivated by your concern for the other person in your relationship.

Patience

And now we come to an idea that I've already introduced into the conversation: patience. Elon Musk once said in an interview, "Patience is a virtue, and I'm learning patience. It's a tough lesson." Musk correctly identified patience as a virtue, whether he knew its source or not. Virtue, in this context, is a practice of moral goodness. In a Scriptural context, the definition of virtue is refined to mean the practice of God's truth.

The word patience is found over thirty times in the New Testament Scriptures. I heard a saying growing up: "Cleanliness is next to godliness." I often heard it when someone encouraged me to clean up as a young boy. But the thing that is next to godliness in scripture is patience. Quoting part of Second Peter, "...add to your faith virtue; and to virtue knowledge; and to knowledge temperance; and to temperance patience; and to patience godliness." The command here is to build on your faith, first practice the truth of God you know, then add to the knowledge (by studying scripture), then allow added knowledge to affect your life by being temperate, then add patience to your moderation, and you can begin to take on godliness. So, it is patience that is next to godliness.

Why is patience given such importance? It is the quality that allows you to endure hardships, trials, and life's disappointments. Whether we like it or not, life will present its share of difficulties to every person. From a Christian perspective, those hardships allow us to develop patience and, thus, godliness. Godliness can be defined as having a good relationship with God.

Bringing this into everyday life, it is patience that allows us to stay calm in the face of any disappointment. It will enable us to think clearly even when things aren't going as we'd like. It's an invaluable part of maintaining healthy relationships. Without patience, we'll lack calm when facing disappointments, meaning our emotions take over our thinking. We've already established that this condition is a terrible place for our mental health.

Elon Musk was also correct that it's a tough lesson. It's not easy to develop patience. After all, it cannot be developed without the presence of disappointment. The little tests of patience the book subjected you to were mild. There are much tougher tests to endure. Disappointment in relationships is one of those harsher lessons.

Contentment

Closely associated with patience is the ability to detach from our ideals. We all have an ideal way we'd like our life to unfold. Chances are we will not realize all of those ideals. Some of our ideas of what is perfect may not even be the best thing for us. But we tend to cling to those ideals despite any logical argument against them. It's a fact of who we are as humans. At times, it's in our best interest to be willing to detach from our ideals, but it takes a quality that is not natural to most humans: contentment. The book of I Timothy tells us, "Godliness with contentment is great gain." Remember that godliness is all about having a good relationship with God. If you realize this, it opens up the meaning of contentment in a relationship. It tells you you'll benefit from this relationship if you are content. This idea of detaching or having contentment is another necessary component of a good relationship.

Let me give you an example of this near the beginning of my relationship with my wife. It was in preparation for our wedding.

Nearly every woman has a picture in her mind of her ideal wedding ceremony. My wife was no different. Jenny had fantasized about every detail of her wedding. Some fantasies weren't practical, as in all fantasies, but some were definitely within reach. One of those dreams included a specific pair of open-toe shoes, an elegant pair with a two-inch heel.

Now, I'm not a tall man, and I had endured many taunting sessions as a teenager, which challenged my manhood because of my height. I had successfully defended myself against the more physical encounters. So, I was a bit sensitive about my height.

Jenny was average height for most women she grew up around, so she and I were comparable in altitudinal stature. However, if Jenny wore those shoes with a two-inch heel, and I wore my dress shoes, she would gain over an inch on my height. When I learned of Jenny's shoe choice, my mind went to exaggeration land, and my mind saw Jenny towering over me in imaginary keepsake photographs of the wedding.

Given my sensitivity to my altitudinal challenges, I spoke to Jenny about her shoe choice. Since the wedding was only a couple of months away, and we would be pretty busy in the time leading up to the wedding, the shoe choice was pretty much set in stone, so I didn't have much hope of changing her mind. Still, I thought it might be best if I confided in her. To my surprise, she didn't resist the change; instead, she stated that every other wedding shoe she investigated had sizeable heels. But I knew she had fallen in love with the ones she chose. They were her ideal shoe choice.

The remarkable thing that struck me then was that she was readily willing to detach herself from her ideal shoe. This willingness, more than anything other thing before we were married, cemented my love for her. It was obvious that she had chosen to accept me, flaws and all, with no reservations. I married up when I married Jenny. She was a better person than me when we were married and still is to this day.

That's not the end of the story. Because all the traditional wedding shoes would have the same problem to a varying degree, Jenny asked me what I suggested. I have no idea where my suggestion had its origin, but my mind produced the only elegant shoe with which I was acquainted that I knew had no heel, the ballerina slipper.

It was a silly, desperate suggestion, but Jenny said, "I'll see if my mom can find a pair before the wedding." No laughing, or no chiding, no judgment, just a willingness to detach and replace her ideal for mine, no matter how ridiculous the suggestion.

Jenny proudly wore the slippers on our wedding day. To this day, whenever I think of us as a couple, as

Kenny and Jenny, I think of those shoes. The shoes symbolized her bond to me, perhaps more important than the wedding ring: a symbol that she chose me over herself. I have been striving to be worthy of her ever since.

This event illustrates what detachment is in a relationship. It's the ability to give up our ideal and substitute it for another person's ideal or a compromise of the two ideals. It is a decision that this person is worth more to me than my ideal. It is where true love begins. This willingness to be content in a relationship is a crucial piece that overthinking takes from us.

If you're ready to take action, there are some steps that you can take to eliminate the habit of reading smoke signals. I've explained the steps to take in another way before, but I like how Alicia Muñoz explains it in her recent book, so I will adapt her explanation to my way of thinking to answer this question.

In the book *Stop Overthinking Your Relationship: Break the Cycle of Anxious Rumination to Nurture Love, Trust, and Connection with Your Partner*, Muñoz describes her SLOW method. It's a catchy little way to remember the steps that I believe will be of benefit.

Remember that impatience and fear, and, in some proportion, doubt play considerable roles in the overthinking mind turning to reading smoke signals. Therefore, it's a good idea to *slow* down the hurry involved and see the *signals* for what they are, bringing us to the *S* in SLOW.

S-L-O-W—See Your Thoughts

> *The scientists of today think deeply instead of clearly. One must be sane to think clearly, but one can think deeply and be quite insane.*
> —Nikola Tesla

Tesla's main complaint about the state of science in the early 1900s is even more valid today. There's been an expansion of the theoretical disciplines compared to the practical disciplines. Some of the ruminations of the theoretical side have led to favoring fanciful storytelling over sound reasoning. Most of us have experienced the storytelling style of teaching science in school to some degree or another. This propensity toward conjecturing to the point of fantasy was something that Tesla distrusted and spoke out against.

If fantasy can creep into a discipline purported to search for knowledge (the Latin root of the word means "to know") using observable facts, how much more easily can fantasy creep into our thoughts about less tangible subject matter?

Seeing your thoughts is about objectively observing our relationship thoughts as if we were a third person outside your relationship. We tend to engage in conjecture about things that we see and experience. It's relatively easy to do.

Below is a picture of a couple beside a body of water. What is going to happen next?

Using your conjecturing abilities, create a brief narrative about what is happening in this picture based on each one of these particular moods: Playful, Happy, and Caring.

Write down each narrative on paper or use the space provided in the *Moving Beyond Overthinking in Relationships Workbook.*

Now, think about what you feel about the young man and the young woman in each scenario that your mind created. Did you make any opinions about the character of each person in this relationship according to the mood you applied to the picture? Did the spirit in which you envisioned this scene change your opinions?

The fact is this picture is just representative of a moment in time. We don't know what image the next moment might give us. Trying to predict it is pointless because we don't know enough about the circumstances of this moment to make an informed decision. Still, that doesn't stop our mind from conjecturing.

In this sort of fun exercise, we were conjecturing about a couple we don't know and upon whom our conjecturing has no consequence. It's a bit different when we engage in conjecture within a relationship that we care about.

Seeing your thoughts is the opposite of multitasking. Doing several things simultaneously without giving them your full attention is the norm in our technology-driven society. It's not unusual to search social media on your phone while watching television. You could be writing an email on your laptop while reminding someone to do a particular task before they leave for the day. Your focus isn't totally on either activity, but you are somewhat aware of the message you're typing and the message you're verbalizing.

To see your thoughts, you have to be focused. It's the sort of concentration one used to put into handwriting a letter when every stroke had a certain level of purpose. Focusing on a single thought you experience in reaction to a visual or experiential cue is like being in a room with a flashlight, searching each nook and cranny individually instead of flipping on an overhead light to reveal the whole room.

Stop what you're doing and concentrate on that thought about your relationship partner without attaching any emotion or mood to it. Once you've put your flashlight on that one thought, ask yourself if this is just a conjecture of your mind. If the answer is "no," then you are saying that this thing in your mind is a fact supported by evidence, and you can act upon it. If your answer is "yes," the thought is just a conjecture of your mind and should be dismissed. If you're unsure, be still again and replay the thought until you are sure of its context.

Let's say your spouse doesn't respond to an action that usually elicits a positive reaction, like a smile or a hug. Conjectures you might have is, *Is he or she mad at me? Did I do something wrong?* But upon reflection, you realize that your spouse didn't recoil from your embrace or show any negative sign. They merely didn't respond. Is there any reason to automatically dwell on this negative conjecture? The answer should be no.

Regarding charity, the type of love that should be in our relationship to others, the scripture says it "thinketh no evil." In other words, love doesn't apply a negative conjecture to others. So stop and focus on those negative inclinations. It's the first step in preventing them.

S-**L**-O-W—Label the Thoughts

> *Complete objectivity is not an option. We are all subjective about the way we respond to 'what is,' whether it's the people we encounter, the circumstances in our lives, or ourselves. What we can do is reduce our subjectivity - what I call 'I see, therefore it is.'*
> —Elizabeth Thornton

We'd all like to think that we're objective in how we see the world around us, but none of us see it the same way, do we? If city dwellers were on vacation taking a walk in farm country and saw a fox trotting across a field, they might be inclined to take out a phone and snap a picture to show their friends the cute little fox they saw on vacation. That same fox would be viewed very differently by a nearby farmer who raised chickens as part of his living. The farmer would see the fox as a threat to his chickens or the eggs his hens lay. The farmer would see the fox as anything but cute. It's the same fox seen from different points of view.

Both the city dwellers and the farmer have opinions about the fox. The city dwellers view the fox as a cute novelty because they don't often see a fox, and the fox is a handsome animal. They have no experience with foxes, so they judge the fox by its appearance. On the other hand, the farmer has had experience with the fox and knows that the fox is fond of eggs and sometimes chicken meat if a chicken is isolated from the others. Therefore, his opinion of the fox is not based solely on appearance but on experience with foxes.

Both views of the fox have evidence to back them up. The fox is a handsome animal, and the people from the city have pictures to back it up, so their opinion of the fox is a fact to them. The farmer has experience evidence to support his view of the fox. He knows a fox wouldn't venture out in the open without reason. Based on experience, he can predict that a desire for a particular food drives the fox, or he wouldn't expose himself by crossing an open field. The farmer's view is a fact to the farmer, just as it is for the city dwellers.

Therefore, both views have elements of objectivity, and both have elements of subjectivity. In this case, both views have validity and, therefore, can be called facts. But that's not always the case with opinions.

For example, look at the man in the following picture and then read the scenarios after the image and think about what might be going through your mind. For each scenario, jot down your thoughts on a separate paper or in the *Moving Beyond Overthinking in Relationships Workbook.*

Moving Beyond Overthinking in Relationships

Scenario 1: You're walking alone on the same path as this man approaches from the opposite direction.

Scenario 2: You're walking with a friend on the same path as this man approaches from the opposite direction.

Scenario 3: You're on a bus with other people and you see this man walking as the bus passes by.

You have slightly different thoughts about the approaching man if you successfully put yourself into the three scenarios. In scenario 1, fear might have tainted your ideas of the man's intentions toward you. The man's appearance is rough, and what might be in the sack he is carrying is unknown. In scenario 2, your thoughts might have had less fear, but the dirty appearance and smell of the man might have led your thoughts in a more judgmental direction. The most objective view you had of the man was probably in scenario 3 because the chance of personal interaction with the man was unlikely.

In reality, this picture was taken in a different country. This man was coming home from a long day's work. He is carrying the fruits of his labor in his sack: enough food to feed his family for the day. He is a good father and a family man through and through. His sole focus was getting home to his family.

How did reality stack up with your view of the man? Were you close in any of the scenarios? If you were close, you managed to see more objectively than subjectively. That is the goal when labeling your thoughts—to be as objective as humanly possible. Put yourself in that bus and view your thoughts from an onlooker's perspective the next time you feel strong negative emotions attached to a thought.

Fact or Pseudo-fact

The first thing that you want to observe about the thought is if it's a fact or a pseudo-fact masquerading as a fact. As we have observed in the example of the fox, facts have evidence to support them. Although the city dwellers may not have had enough information to understand the significance of the fox crossing an open field, their observation never went beyond the fox's appearance, so the thought that the fox was cute was factual. The farmer's observation about the fox's motive was also valid because of his many encounters with foxes. His thinking could go beyond the appearance of the fox directly to its motive.

While we can successfully predict the motives of wild animals when we have sufficient information about their behaviors in their natural environment, the motives of people aren't so predictable. Humans are rational, reasoning creatures with a great capacity for emotion. It's a complex mixture that can result in unexpected reactions to outside and internally-generated stimuli.

In a close relationship, we often feel that we have come to understand our partner and can predict how they will react to us. However, there are so many variables in how humans express their state of mind that our predictions are often wrong.

My wife, Jenny, can be somewhat reserved at times, and she is very vibrant at other times. After only a few months of marriage, there was a noticeable shift in Jenny toward the reserved side. I was constantly mistaking her reserved behavior as denoting dissatisfaction within our relationship. Sometimes, I was right, but many times I was wrong. Later on, I learned that her reserved state was her default state. She is reserved most of the time when she is living her everyday life. But she can be very vibrant at other times. For example, she will be very enthusiastic when anticipating something different than the usual humdrum of life. Right now, a trigger for her to be her vibrant self could be an approaching trip to see the grandchildren.

Before I caught onto the reserved nature being a default, I would wonder what I might have done wrong. No matter how often she assured me that nothing was wrong, I still wasn't convinced. I just knew there was something between us.

I was viewing her lack of vibrancy as something unusual, therefore indicating some dissatisfaction on her part. I didn't have enough information to predict her behavior, so my observations were tainted with emotional subjectivity. I was creating facts out of my thoughts about her when, in fact, my thoughts were pseudo-facts. They were based on my expectations, not on objective evidence.

Learning to examine our thoughts from a distance, apart from the emotion influencing them, is the first step in learning to slow down and look at our thoughts.

The next step is determining whether the thought is a fact or a pseudo-fact. Pseudo-facts are created in four primary ways. They can be an assumption, like the example of Jenny and I in our early marriage. They can be opinions, which can either be informed or uninformed. If it's an informed opinion, it could be upgraded to a fact if the information you know is correct. Uninformed opinions, however, have a high probability of being a pseudo-fact. We've covered this somewhat already with the example of the foxes and the three scenarios concerning the picture of the man.

Another way pseudo-facts are formed in our minds is the making of judgments. It is possible that you made some judgments about the man in the picture. It's perfectly natural if you did. Our mind scans our surroundings for potential threats. If the man brought a sense of fear to our minds, it is because we judged the man capable of causing us harm. Your mind would have mere moments to assess the man and prepare for a possible threat. However, having judgments in response to a potential threat and having judgments in a relationship are two different things. Negative judgments of a partner's character will bleed into your mind whenever you perceive an adverse action or reaction. You'll also be more apt to see negative elements in your spouse even when their actions or reactions are neutral or harmless. This is not a good place to be in any relationship.

In a relationship, the fear is less easy to qualify. Fears would be associated with the relationship: the fear of being emotionally hurt, a fear of commitment, or a fear of harming the relationship are examples. Assumptions are the last of the ways we develop pseudo-facts. Fears that negative assumptions breed feed blanket assumptions. A blanket assumption is when a particular fear makes you assume a specific motivation behind your personal interactions. In a dating relationship, you might attach a rationale behind your dating partner's desire to spend time with friends instead of you on a given evening. In a marriage, you might wonder why your wife or husband can talk so freely on a phone call with their mother or brother when conversations between you and your spouse can be laborious. In both cases, your partner probably wants to reconnect with older relationships that have been neglected because you both spend most of your time with each other.

So, we see that pseudo-facts can come from opinions, expectations, assumptions, and judgments, the most harmful of which are negative judgments. It's essential to understand whether the thought you're harboring in your mind is a fact or a false fact, a pseudo-fact. Pseudo-facts do not merit our mind's attention and should be dismissed out of your mind as you would toss out spoiled food. Neither is worthy of your consumption.

Overthinking Cycles

Let's review the different overthinking or ruminating cycles that tend to occur. There is a cycle that produces thoughts that tend to assign blame either to yourself or to your partner. We called it the Blame Game Cycle. This cycle's thoughts create selective memories that support the assignation of blame that your mind has concocted. Another persistent cycle is the Self-pity Cycle. In these ruminations, you are always the victim. Then there's the Worry Cycle, where worst-case scenarios rule. It's the ultimate indulgence of the old making a mountain out of a molehill scenario. The Control Freak Cycle thoughts all assert that you know best and are the only one who knows what to do in a given or multiple situations. And finally, the Doubt Trip Cycle in which your insecurities are allowed to overcome any rational thought. Even if there's ample evidence of your partner's commitment to you, there will be an avalanche of thoughts that will undermine the facts you see. The phrase, "It's too good to be true," creates a new meaning in your mind. You can experience any or all of these types of thoughts in a rumination cycle.

Rumination is an intriguing term. It comes from the observation of grazing animals. When a cow chews its cud, the cow is ruminating. A cow's digestive system functions much better the more the cow ruminates or chews its cud. A rumination cycle in a cow has four stages: regurgitation of feed, rechewing, resalivation, and reswallowing. That sounds gross to us, but it benefits the cow immensely. Alternately, suppose a cow is not allowed to rest after feeding because it is agitated by some environmental factor or disease. In that case, a cow can become extremely sick because it won't ruminate. The more rumination, the better for the cow.

Conversely, repeated rumination of thoughts in our mind, the constant regurgitation of thoughts and thought patterns, can be very unhealthy. But let me qualify that statement. Suppose the bringing back of a course of thought is only for problem-solving, such as solving a math theorem, a problem at work, or another issue in life, without attaching negative emotions. In that instance, this form of exercise is good for the mind. However, even if the rumination is benign, such as solving a math problem, constant rumination without resolution can lead to frustrations that ignite negative emotions.

Now, consider that the original thought of the rumination was emotionally negative at its inception.

When your mind regurgitates the thought, you experience the negativity of the original thought all over again—trying to resolve that perceived issue, which is not factually based at the outset, results in frustration because rational thought cannot resolve an irrational issue. The more the cycle regurgitates, the more negative emotions pile up within the mind, inhibiting any rationality that remains connected to that cycle. Soon, you can't think your way out of a paper bag.

That's why it's so important to understand a pseudo-fact at its conception. It's also important to understand why thoughts further along in a rumination cycle are now in your mind. If we learn to label the cycle, we will understand why our mind produces those thoughts even though they may have morphed considerably from the original thought.

Let's use an example of a fictional couple to see if we understand the labeling process.

Lisa and Melvin have been married for a little over a year, but both tend to overthink. One day, Melvin noticed that Lisa had mismatched the socks in his drawer. He must get dressed in the dark in the mornings, so he matches up the socks.

At supper, Lisa makes his favorite dish. It was delicious, but he failed to thank her for it. After supper, Melvin sees that a spoon was left on the table, so he puts the spoon in the dishwasher and notices that two dishes are nearly on top of each other, so he rearranges them slightly to provide more space between them. Lisa noticed and frowned, but Melvin didn't see the frown.

Later that evening, Lisa is watching a game show when a baseball game featuring Melvin's favorite team is on. Melvin had mentioned the game in passing the night before. They have a loud argument over what to watch on television, and both get angry at one another.

What might have been happening in Melvin's and Lisa's minds to cause this anger? What pseudo-facts were introduced into Melvin's thinking? What pseudo-facts were introduced into Lisa's thinking? What rumination cycle or cycles might have been at work in their minds? What could have been done to avoid the fight?

Some possible pseudo-facts and cycles for this scenario, as well as the introduction of other scenarios, are provided in the *Moving Beyond Overthinking in Relationships Workbook*.

S-L-**O**-W—Open to the Present

One of the crucial problems overthinking presents is the inability to focus on the here and now. The first two steps of SLOW ask you to focus on the thoughts that you are currently having as you feel a bout of negative rumination about to start. It's not easy because of the emotion that attaches itself to the thoughts, triggering that longing for that familiar hormonal high that the beginning of an overthinking cycle can bring. Too often, your mind so easily conjures up thoughts about troublesome past events or future worries when an unsettling thought invades your mind.

If while trying to focus on that disturbing thought or set of thoughts, you catch your mind conjuring up past events or future unknowns related to the thought or thoughts, stop yourself by closing your eyes and focus them on the darkness you see, and then take a deep breath or two. Once you've calmed your mind, open your eyes and look around at your surroundings. If you're inside, take in the color and textures of the walls, and patterns that might be in the floor or ceilings, or count the number of windows you see. If you're outside, see what is actually around you. Is there more of one kind of tree than another? Are there any birds chirping? The point is, wherever you are, take in what is around you until the dopamine, adrenaline, serotonin, and cortisol dissipate, and your mind stops doing that familiar dance toward looping. If you become still enough to consider the trigger and thoughts that began that dance, go back and try to see the thoughts for what they actually are and give them a label. Once that is done, bring yourself back to the present immediately and go on with your business of life.

There can be times when it's more challenging to bring yourself back to the present. Perhaps it is because you were also doing something else while trying to focus on that thought. You haven't focused your mind on any one thing, and therefore, it becomes more difficult to gain the single focus that is needed to get back to the present. If you tend to be a multitasker, you must eliminate other tasks while trying the SLOW method intentionally. If you're at work, and you keep a beverage at your desk or near your work area, take a sip and close your eyes when you are triggered to start overthinking. This action will allow you to only focus on the thought, see it, and label it. It only takes a moment, so take that moment, then begin doing your work again.

Another thing that can limit your ability to be in the present is social media or other distractions that might exist on your phone. If you find yourself constantly fiddling with your phone when you could be involved with other people in your surroundings, you're making yourself susceptible to letting your mind wander. If your mind wanders, you lose focus. If you lose focus, you lose the present and start living in the past and future—the domain of overthinking. Don't live there. Limit your phone time and spend more time in the present. Living in the present exercises your mind without the harmful side effects.

Stop Trying to Read Smoke Signals

If you're alone, don't default to some technology to entertain yourself. Using alone time constructively is possible instead of being a detriment. Be mindful of your surroundings. Focus on something. Don't let your mind wander. Close your eyes and listen. Focus on the sounds. Do you hear something you didn't notice with your eyes open? Reading can be very beneficial to your mind during your alone time. But don't focus your reading on negative things like the news or a book that might encourage strong negative reactions from your mind. A hobby in which you work with your hands can also be beneficial. Do activities that require you to focus.

Overthinking is the opposite of focus; it demands that your mind wander hither and yon, trying to find that elusive resolution that never comes. It is a looping of mindlessness, a spiral of negative thinking. Train your mind to focus on the present instead.

If you aren't in the moment, you are either looking forward to uncertainty, or back to pain and regret.
—*Jim Carrey*

S-L-O-**W**—Welcome the Unknown

There's an old saying, "What you don't know can't hurt you." It's an adage to encourage people to move on with their plans and look optimistically toward the future. It's been years since I've heard anyone use that phrase.

Rather often, I've seen the underlying meaning, if not the exact words of the opposite of that phrase: "What you don't know can hurt you." It's in advertising all the time. Do you know what that *thing,* whatever it is, causes this *terrible problem*, whatever that is? This *product*, whatever it is, can solve that *problem* that you didn't know that you had.

That thought has also surfaced in many so-called watchdog groups that have sprung up over the years. Even the news encourages viewership with slogans like "Be in the Know."

Has the increase of this opposite mantra contributed to the rise in the occurrences of overthinking manifesting itself today? It's nothing that can be tracked statistically. One can observe that overthinking is a growing problem in our society. One can also observe that society as a whole is being manipulated into thinking that not knowing something is bad, really bad, regardless of whether not knowing a particular thing is bad at all in and of itself. The two trends do seem to mirror each other.

I want to do a little reinforcing of that adage. It's okay not to know. How boring life would be if we really did know everything. Suppose we woke up in the morning and knew exactly how our day would unfold, and we knew every action and reaction that people would have that day. For a few days, that might be marvelous. But after a while, living in such a world would be akin to living in a computer-generated scenario. Even with AI development, there would only be so many variables that a person could encounter. All of those variables would have to follow a certain logic. The lack of uncertainty, the illogical, if you will, would be noticeable. The logical end of that type of existence would be a definite lack of purpose for all characters involved in that scenario.

Not knowing is good. The Swiss philosopher Henri Frederic Amiel wrote on more than one occasion, "Uncertainty is the refuge of hope." That statement seems backward, doesn't it? Don't we think of hope as the refuge when we feel uncertain? Yet Amiel said that it is uncertainty that is the refuge. Focus on that thought. Why would uncertainty be a place of safety Read the quote again. It's not *our* place of safety. It's *hope's* refuge. In other words, uncertainty is the place where hope is safe; it's the place that secures hope's future. Without uncertainty, there would be no hope. There would be none of hope's anticipation. There would be none of hope's fulfillment. There would be nothing to strive to attain if everything was sure. Therefore, uncertainty is necessary to build one of the most essential living elements: hope.

Let your hope shape your future, not your doubts, not your fears, not your hurts. We need to remove the doubt of uncertainty, the fear of the unknown, and the hurts of the past from our lives so that hope can reign supreme. A hope-filled life is a healthy, purposeful life.

Uncertainty, the unknown, should be embraced, not tucked away in a dark corner of our mind. It should be what drives us to better ourselves. Faith and hope walk hand in hand. Without uncertainty, there would be no need for faith in each other, in ourselves, or God. Faith is what strengthens our hope. We all have faith in something; we would have no hope if we didn't. A person incapable of hope is a person beyond helping. People that can't hope have only despair.

Another old adage varies depending on whether you're a man or a woman. "Women, you can't live with them, and you can't live without them." Or, "Men, you can't live with them, and you can't live without them." This maxim speaks to the differences between men and women. Sometimes, these differences can be frustrating and annoying. Other times, these differences are comforting and complementary.

Let's apply that same saying to uncertainty. At times, everyone has a hard time with not knowing. Some folks just can't live with uncertainty. It haunts them to the point of vexation through overthinking. But no one can live without uncertainty. Facing the unknown is what makes us thrive in both faith and hope. It makes life worth living.

Since uncertainty in relationships and the future vexes the overthinker, they have many thoughts that center on the doubt caused by that vexation. Sometimes, these thoughts have no actual external trigger. They just pop into our conscious thoughts because they are readily available in our subconscious minds due to the vast amount of time and energy wasted ruminating about them. These random thoughts become our internal triggers to ruminate. Sometimes, the mere presence of the thought can trigger another negative emotional thought about ourselves or others. Then these thoughts trigger other thoughts, and off we go again on that rumination rollercoaster.

Therefore, it's important to welcome these unwelcome thoughts. I know that sounds like double talk but consider the following picture.

Can this tiger hurt you? If you were standing before this tiger snapping this picture, the answer to this question is an emphatic *Yes!*

Now consider this question: Can this picture hurt you? The answer to that would be a sniggering, *no, of course not!*

Thoughts, especially those with no basis in truth, are just thoughts. They have only the power we give to them. Rob them of their power by welcoming them into our conscious thought by treating them like the picture of the lion. You know what they represent and the pain they've caused you and those around you, but they are not real; they are only an afterimage of the mind. They can't hurt you unless you make them real to you. Making them real in your mind can make them real in your actions, and those thoughts become your reality. It's like the tiger. If it's really in front of you, you're in danger; if it's only an image, you can look at the tiger and admire its beauty because no harm can come to you.

Here's the key thought. View your thoughts without attaching emotion to them. It's the negative emotions that are fueling and controlling your overthinking in relationships. It's time to see them for what they are—thoughts, nothing more.

The Big Picture of SLOW

SLOW is a method that relies on you to tell reality from detrimental imaginings. Whether it is an external or internal trigger that causes a negative thought to surface in your mind, resist restarting the rumination process. Instead, see the thought for what it really is and label it. Be in the present as you do this; don't drift back into the arms of overthinking that comforts for a short time only to grip you like a vice. After you've understood precisely what the thought is, make it an image to be viewed without negative emotions and leave the tiger to its own imaginary territory while you stay in reality. Don't grab the tiger's tail and get pulled into territory where you can get hurt.

> *I have realized that the past and future are real illusions, that they exist in the present, which is what there is and all there is.*
> —Alan Watts

If you find this book worthwhile so far, please leave a review on Amazon. Your few sentences could be the encouragement someone needs to change their life.

Get Off the Rumination Rollercoaster
◆◆◆

Rollercoasters are fun. That statement alone is enough to get Jenny to react negatively if she thinks there's any chance of her riding one.

Jenny has a fear of heights that is palpable. The mere thought of climbing something high is enough to freeze her in her tracks. Before I understood the extent of her phobia, I asked her to ride up the CN Tower with me back when we visited Toronto. Her face went pale, and she sat down, unable to answer me. I sat down beside her, thinking that she was getting ill. After talking with her for a while, I understood the cause of her sudden affliction. It was pure, unadulterated fear. The thought of being so high was enough to nearly put her into shock.

Rollercoasters are high, especially the ones that I enjoyed as a kid. I did get Jenny to ride a lesser rollercoaster that wasn't terribly high—once. That feeling of weightlessness when going down that first hill was terrifying to her, and she never wanted to do it again. So, the analogy of a rollercoaster doesn't quite mean the same thing to my wife as it does to others, myself included.

If you enjoy rollercoasters, the analogy makes more sense. I'm speaking to those who love the anticipation of the slow climb up the first hill, the exhilaration of that first dive down, and the speed at which the following bends in the track are navigated. The desire to *do it again* usually surfaces as soon as that last hairpin turn is made. When I was a kid, I could have ridden the rollercoaster all day. The only downside was the long lines. Those were a drag. At times, the long lines made me want to hunt for a ride that didn't require much waiting.

Overthinking is somewhat like that addictive amusement ride. It reels you in with the promise of motivation, exhilaration, and satisfaction, only to give you a heaping helping of stress as you arduously run through seemingly never-ending loops in your mind. You get to wallow in self-pity, doubt, blame, worry, and disdain. No waiting is needed to take ride after ride, but the thrill is gone soon. Your energy is drained. You feel unfulfilled, and now your body is giving you signs that things aren't okay. Welcome to the Mental Disillusion Park, where the main attraction is the Rumination Rollercoaster.

The bad news is that your overthinking has made you and your relationships miserable. The good news is that you don't have to stay on this rollercoaster; there is a way off.

Discover Your Triggers

> *We are not a victim of our emotions or thoughts. We can understand our triggers and use them as tools to help us respond more objectively.*
> —Elizabeth Thornton

"Only you can prevent forest fires." This was the slogan heard from Smokey the Bear for over fifty years. The USDA Forest Service updated the slogan to "Only you can prevent wildfires" in 2001. The service was trying to make the point that many fires that consume American forests are set by the careless actions of the people who visit them. The slogan was intended to encourage the public to take personal responsibility for their actions concerning their handling of fires when in forested areas. The service wanted everyone to know that the prevention of these fires wasn't just their issue; it was each individual's responsibility.

In the same manner, the prevention of overthinking is something that is an individual's responsibility. Nobody but you can know what sets off an overthinking cycle in your mind.

Returning to our rollercoaster analogy, overthinking or ruminating is like a rollercoaster ride in another way. The ride ends right where it began. Ruminating gets you nowhere, but you still have to pay the cost of the ride. This cost is spent in the currency of energy, time, and pain. The cost is where the analogy no longer applies. You may not mind paying the price of admission to ride a rollercoaster since it's not something you do all that often. However, ruminating is a ride you take all the time, so this ride adds up to a tremendous cost over time.

"Only you can prevent overthinking cycles." These costly cycles rob you of precious time and energy. They lead nowhere and can cause you and others great pain. It's up to you to stop them.

This brings us to the topic of triggers. A trigger is anything that sparks intense negative emotions. It could be a memory, an event, an object, or a person. It could be just a random thought that doesn't come from a known source. It can be literally anything. Since triggers can come in many forms, it would be like playing darts in the dark for me to be able to list your specific triggers in this book. I might get lucky and hit a bullseye for you, but let's not leave this up to a lucky shot.

Instead, let's concentrate on identifying the moment of your trigger. That moment when your mind gets troubled, your body reacts, and you begin to desire to ruminate. If you have the problem of overthinking, you are familiar with the moment I've just described. You go from feeling fine to having a feeling in the pit of your stomach. It is a tight feeling that isn't full-blown nausea but gives you a sinking feeling. It's a gnawing at your mind that all is not well anymore. It's a flood of negative energy that seems to come from nowhere.

At that moment, something is going through your mind. A reaction to something you saw, heard, smelled, tasted, or felt that created a negative thought that your body can't determine, but it's there in your mind. Or maybe it wasn't your external senses that caused the reaction. Perhaps it was a memory or a random thought that brought it on. This is the moment to act.

Take a deep breath or two. It helps alleviate the tension. Don't let your mind wander to the past or future; stay in the moment and focus your mind on the feeling. Is it anger, is it fear, is it doubt? Find the thought that brought on the feeling. It would be a negative thought. See the thought, identify it, and label it. Know your enemy in that moment.

Know the pattern of thinking that brought that thought to your mind. Was it a thought blaming you or someone else? Was it a thought of something threatening your plans? Was it a thought that cast a shadow of doubt on your mind? Was the thought born out of an unreasonable fear of what might happen? Or was it a thought that made you a victim in some way?

Understand at that moment what the thought was and why you thought it. This kind of understanding of the thought and its cause will lead you directly to the trigger.

Here's another scenario with Melvin and Lisa to give you a practical illustration of the process just described.

Melvin is working in his study late into the evening to meet an approaching deadline at work. Lisa has retired for the night.

Melvin is nearly done with his work, but his mind is getting tired, so he sits back in his chair for a moment to take a short break, feeling pretty good about his evening of work.

It was then that he heard a faint wheezing cough.

Immediately, his good feeling was gone; he had a dread about Lisa that he couldn't reconcile within his mind. It had happened so fast that he nearly fell backward in his chair. As he caught himself, he took a deep breath.

During that breath, it became clear to him what had happened.

He shook his head, smiled, and focused on his work again with new motivation to be finished. He would be with Lisa soon and check on her then.

Without really thinking about it, Melvin had performed the SLOW method. What had really happened in Melvin's mind at that moment in time?

Melvin came back to the present because he nearly lost his balance. It occurred to him that the wheezing cough had triggered a thought about his mother, who had died of emphysema. She had coughed like that at night. He had begun to worry about Lisa without warning and recognized it as a pattern of thinking that had formed overthinking cycles in the past. He dismissed the thought as an unsubstantiated pseudo-thought and used the incident as motivation to finish. Melvin accepted that he would find Lisa well and looked forward to proving that to himself.

This scenario also illustrates why triggers are hard to define in real life. Everyone has their own history of experiences and emotions related to them. It is necessary to have a certain amount of self-awareness to determine triggers. Most of us can pick out specific events in our past that stand out. These events are almost always associated with a strong emotion of some sort. When the feeling is negative, such as in the passing of a loved one, they can become triggers to overthinking. Negativity, in whatever form it takes, is the fuel for overthinking.

Avoiding Triggering Environments

I've stressed the point of the perils of overthinking to the point where you might be thinking: *Okay, Kenny.*

I get it! Overthinking is BAD. But I just can't seem to help myself.

I do understand that. That's why I've emphasized the problems. I appreciate that overthinking can be an emotional drug. It can be addicting. I get you. Let's shift gears to address that.

You realize that overthinking is bad and want to do something about it. You see how the SLOW method can help you with staving off overthinking, but you doubt that it will prevent you from wanting to overthink. Like any addict, although you know the practice is tearing you apart, you still want to return to it. You feel you HAVE to go back to it. Let's talk prevention.

The first step is avoiding situations where your mind is tempted to wander. Again, this revolves around staying in the present most of the time. Just as an alcoholic should avoid keeping liquor handy or going to bars, the overthinker should avoid long periods of idle time, as should everyone, in reality.

Folks in colonial times understood the worthlessness and dangers of idleness. Thomas Jefferson wrote, "Determine never to be idle. No person will have occasion to complain of the want of time who never loses any. It is wonderful how much may be done if we are always doing." Isaac Watts warned, "For Satan always finds some mischief still for idle hands to do." And Benjamin Franklin quipped, "It is the working man who is the happy man. It is the idle man who is the miserable man."

To put it bluntly, if you're not being productive, you're being idle. From personal experience with the following, I can say without reservation that production does not occur when you're flipping through social media pages or fiddling with apps on your phone. You're not being productive when you watch television; believe it or not, you're not being productive when playing video games. All of these so-called activities are not productive.

Your mind longs to be productive. If you spend hours in non-productive activities, it's no wonder your mind desires to have something to do. If you're not providing your mind with enough productive things to do, it will tend to find pseudo-production, and thus, the temptation to begin overthinking occurs.

We stay in the present by doing, not by watching, searching, or engaging in mindless (as in the opposite of mindful), time-consuming activities in which our minds are more spectator than participant. I've played enough video games to know it requires focus, not engagement. It's a matter of reaction rather than resolving. They engage only parts of the mind, not the mind as a whole.

If we use our leisure time productively, our minds will not long as much to be used, if not being useful, in overthinking. The mind will not have as much desire to engage in frivolous use since more productive uses are available.

Again, I'm trying to be as direct as possible in this book. This may take you aback somewhat. But really, the development of certain convenience technologies and the subsequent lessening of the use of the mind for valuable purposes significantly contribute to the rapid rise of overthinking in our society.

Mindset Triggers

So, apart from the lack of productive thinking, are there other reasons for your mind's constant desire to overthink? It's possible. Let's take a look at some of the other contributors.

There is a school of thought that says, "If you want something done right, do it yourself." This school of thinking doesn't trust others to do things but wants to micromanage not only their lives but the lives of others. This can be taken to extremes that cause much anxiety in the people who think this way and those around them. People who tend to feel this way are sometimes called perfectionists. They have the illusion that they can control outcomes.

In professions, if it is one where working alone is necessary, this mindset can excel. The drive to find a way to get a desired outcome can work to their benefit in these professions.

However, in relationships, this sort of thinking discourages closeness or intimacy. This lack of intimacy can cause a callous disregard for other's feelings and needs. In the relationship arena, this person must change their mindset or be prone to overthinking simply because he needs the cooperation of others to get the desired outcome. A mindset stuck in the "it's my way or the highway" mode will struggle endlessly to try to make a relationship work without getting a resolution. This is the most problematic of mindsets for relationships. The relationship itself will be rife with tension and mistrust.

Many successful professionals have problems with relationships. The perfectionist mindset is many times the cause. The perfectionist mind is trained to resolve issues in a way that is good for the profession under their control. However, what is good when flying solo may not always be suitable for a relationship with a copilot. So, the desire to resolve the relationship issues spins into uncontrolled rumination loops that cause a lack of focus that affects the relationship and the profession.

Okay, suppose that this perfectionist mindset is your mindset. Suppose it's worked for you in business or your profession. Why would you want to change it? Is your relationship reason enough? Do you have a fixed mindset, or are you willing to grow?

> *With a fixed mindset, you're so worried about how smart or talented you are, you don't take on challenges. You don't try new things.*
> —Carol S. Dweck

I am again speaking from personal experience. A perfectionist doesn't have to be a perfectionist all the time. Expecting the best out of yourself is the good part of being a perfectionist. It's good to always do your best. However, there is a bad part of being a perfectionist. It's the part that says, "Everyone else has to do it my way or they're just in the way." This is the relationship killer in you. Let's face it: Perfectionists have too high of an opinion of themselves and too low of others.

The following is meant only for the perfectionists among you. Others are welcome to read it, but it's primarily for perfectionists.

> Focusing on a romantic relationship, such as dating or marriage, let me ask you, as a perfectionist, a series of questions about your relationship. Why did you want to have a relationship with this person in the first place? Did it involve anything other than animal lust? If it did affect more than lust, did it include assigning a value to this person? If it involved giving value, is this person worth being in this relationship?
>
> Now, none of those questions should have led you to be in this relationship because something is missing in those questions, isn't there? But they should have been considered. I have to assume that as a rational human being, you think that your partner is worth being in this relationship with you. If he or she is worth being in the relationship, then doesn't that follow that they should have a say in the decisions involving the relationship? Don't you owe them that much consideration?
>
> If you answered yes to these questions, the next step is yours alone. You must make an adjustment to your mindset's negative man-

tra to something akin to this: "My partner's opinions are more important to me than reaching our goals my way. I will value those opinions no matter what my initial reaction tells me about them, and we will reach our goals together."

Mindsets can be altered. It's not easy, but it's imperative to try.

This again reminds me of something relevant from Scripture. Philippians 2:4,5 says, "Look not every man on his own things, but every man also on the things of others. Let this mind be in you, which was also in Christ Jesus." Here, people who hold to the Christian faith are instructed to take on the mindset of Christ Jesus. The Scripture tells us much of this mindset, and it is not an easy task. But those of true faith have a Divine Helper to assist us in this transformation. I'm still working on it with His assistance. But the relevance here is that we are made to be able to change mindsets. It's not an impossible task.

The following mindset is not as personal to me, but it still hinders those seeking to get off the rumination rollercoaster. This is the mindset I call Sympathy Syndrome. Any kind of issue that we might have can bring out sympathy or pity from people around us. This can feel pretty good, and some people begin to use their overthinking issues to garner this good feeling from others. Overthinkers have a way of finding the cloud in every silver lining to reverse a common saying, and they'll use these clouds to rain on other people's parades. During these little showers of distress, the thoughts that they've internalized over time are sprinkled out on their friends. As long as their friends try to give them sympathy or pity in return, it serves as a catalyst to continue the overthinking cycles and offers them at least partial payment for the next rollercoaster ride.

This mindset is of an oversharing nature. Oversharing folks simply share everything that's on their mind. It can stem from a nervous habit or be purposeful to push away any chance of intimacy. It can result from loneliness or merely not knowing what else to say, a sort of social hang-up akin to extreme introversion but manifested oppositely.

However, in the overthinking mind, it is something different. When rumination can be identified with a self-pity cycle, the overthinking mind embraces the role of the victim, a phenomenon that is not as rare in our current culture as it used to be. This victimhood requires retribution in this mindset, and their friends are paying for it. This mindset rationalizes that other people need to understand their plight. Oversharing serves a dual purpose: one of retribution and one of restoration in the form of sympathy, which fuels their desire to repeat the cycle.

Changing this mindset is no easier than any other, but it is pretty clear how to begin. The writer Richard Bach put it this way, "If it's never our fault, we can't take responsibility for it. If we can't take responsibility for it, we'll always be its victim." This never-ending cycle is irresponsible. (Okay, I couldn't resist the pun, a weakness of mine.) But in reality, it's true. When things go wrong in our lives, it's easy to point the finger at someone or something else. It's much harder to take at least some responsibility upon ourselves. But I suppose the easiest way to escape the victimhood cycle is to learn to forgive people. If you forgive people, you are no longer under the power of victimhood.

A principle concerning forgiveness is related well in Psalm 32: "Blessed is he whose transgression is forgiven, whose sin is covered." When a trespass, a wrong against a fellow human, is forgiven, the result is a covering of the sin or the offense against God. When God forgives, it is like that act never happened. This is the same principle of forgiveness for us. This is why when

Peter asked Jesus how many times a man should forgive and suggested seven times, Jesus answered, "I say not unto thee, Until seven times: but, Until seventy times seven." I could go into the significance of seven in the Scripture, but the important part here is the idea that you simply forgive forever. Forgiveness is forever.

If you can learn to truly forgive, you are covering that offense as if it never happened with no limit in mind or forever. How can you be a victim if no wrong is committed against you?

The last big issue facing an overthinking mind is a hybrid mindset mixing the doubt and worry cycles. Both doubt and worry are fueled by fear of the future. Doubt is a fear of what won't happen, and worry is a fear of what will happen. In a relationship, this dual mindset is often manifested by a fear of conflict. As some of our scenarios in our workbook and, perhaps, some of your own experiences bear out, a fear of conflict only leads to other discords that are more serious in nature. Therefore, the fear itself is the cause of more reason to fear conflict.

Unlike the other mindsets discussed in this chapter, this mindset is a product of overthinking, not a preexisting mindset. It is genuinely a self-replicating mindset that only deepens as doubt and worry cycles continue in the mind.

Regarding a relationship, doubt shows a lack of trust in your partner. It is the idea that your partner might have less than sincere motives. Worry is the result of concern that some attitude or bond in your partner will change, and the change will be detrimental to the relationship. Both produce a fear of confronting the partner when a perceived wrong has been done, or when a decision is made that appears to violate an established agreement between the partners. Doubt comes into play when an immediate adverse reaction is expected, and worry is more about the concern of future reprisals due to a change in your partner.

I guess this mindset can be referenced as the mistrustful mindset, as that is at the core of the perspective. If you really trust your partner, there would be no fear of conflict. Sure, there would be a slight fear of disappointing someone you genuinely care about. Still, if your relationship is built on trust, the fear of the consequences of not letting your partner know about a relatively minor disappointment would be more significant.

Trust must be earned, but how can it be earned if there is no original trust to prove or disprove? A relationship must have a foundation of trust, or there will be nothing on which to build a deeper trust.

Stephen Covey puts it this way, "Trust is the glue of life. It's the most essential ingredient in effective communication. It's the foundational principle that holds all relationships."

This mindset has to be overcome by taking that first step of commitment. Take small steps toward trust, taking the first steps toward reconciliation should any friction develop. Don't wait for your partner to reconcile with you; you take the first step and see how your partner reacts. If there is any foundation of trust, it will be strengthened by your actions, and you will gradually lose the need for fear to protect yourself.

That's the way any meaningful relationship starts with a willingness to take that first step of trust, or faith, if you will. That's the way a Christian's relationship with God begins. We take that first step to God, and then that relationship removes our fear. "For God hath not given us the spirit of fear; but of power, and of love, and of a sound mind." II Timothy 1:7

We started this chapter by discussing past events as triggers for overthinking. But past events are different in a healthy mind. Emotions connected with the events can be good, healthy emotions instead of harmful. The events associated with good emotions can also be triggers, but they can act as an encouragement instead of a detriment. This is why people who have a healthy mind remember the past fondly. The bad things are relegated to obscurity, and the mind focuses on the good things that happened.

Folks who dwell on the negative tend to have mental issues. This is another motivation to limit the overthinking cycles in our lives. The more your mind focuses on the negative, the more problems it can cause you and those around you.

Showing Gratitude

I mentioned a German study on gratitude earlier in the book. I don't want to bog you down with too many details, but I'll give you the gist of the study here.

The study was conducted over seven years on 70 couples. Ten of the 70 couples were selected to participate in the study for a year. The study repeated the process for seven years with a different set of ten couples. These couples were chosen because at least one person in each pair had problems with anxiousness in their relationships. The study commenced with interviews of each person designed to determine their view on the quality of their relationship. The individual partners rated all the relationships at the lower end of the quality scale. This was the baseline of the study.

The couples were asked to think of a way to show gratitude for their partner daily. Other than that request, no relationship counseling was done. Each person kept a journal to track how they felt about their relationship interactions for each day. Each couple was assigned a specific time of the month to meet with the researchers to discuss their relationships.

Here are the findings of the study. The journal entries revealed that when gratitude was shown to them, positive emotions were felt by each participant. As the research progressed, it was noted that the positive entries in the journals began to outweigh the negative entries for most couples. The couples where no real difference was seen in this context were couples that didn't show gratitude each day but only sporadically. At the end of the year, the pairs were interviewed again to determine the quality of their relationships. According to their journals, the couples that showed gratitude more often were those whose relationship ratings improved dramatically. The duos that showed gratitude less often either showed no improvement or improved only slightly. The study also showed that those whose relationship ratings improved dramatically also reduced their tendency toward anxious behavior.

This study shows clinical evidence of something that can be observed in our everyday lives. If someone offers you kindness or gratitude during the day, what emotions does it elicit from you? After receiving a compliment or experiencing benevolence, how does it affect how you view the next person you meet?

The study showed that an attitude of gratitude was contagious. The more gratitude was practiced, the more gratitude was reciprocated. This is deduced from the increase in the ratio of positive to negative journal entries. The study revealed that gratitude is also a formidable weapon to use against anxiousness. It changed the way the couples viewed their relationship in a very favorable way.

Could showing gratitude to your partner improve your relationship? The study says *yes.* If the quality of your relationship improves, would that reduce the temptation to overthink your relationship? Logic says *yes.* Will showing gratitude cure all your relationship ills? No, but it is a massive step in the right direction.

The truth is gratitude does not come naturally to us humans. We have to have it trained into us as children; no child comes into this world with an attitude of gratitude. How many parents have said, "Say thank you" to their young children hundreds of times before the lesson takes hold? *Many.* And even when the child is trained to thank people for things they do for them, how many children are sincere in their gratitude? There's no precise way of knowing until you see how they behave when they grow up. There is something that can help in parenting, and it's simply this thought. Children tend to mimic what they see in you. Do you show gratitude to your children?

Genuine gratitude has to be nurtured into existence. It's not a matter of a mental assertion that creates it. It has to come from the heart, or in other words, your soul. Deep down, you must be grateful for gratitude to show its total sincerity. Once ingrained in your soul, it will come out in practice without any mental assertion.

A relationship is one of the best ways to show and nurture gratitude. When both partners are genuinely grateful for each other, it is noticeable in a relationship. The intrinsic difference in such a relationship can transform the nature of both people in that relationship.

Gratitude, or a spirit of thanksgiving, is mentioned over a hundred times in scripture. It plays a vital role in the life of faith. That's because the life of faith is all about a relationship, that is, a relationship with God. If God values it enough to mention it often, how much value does it have in a relationship? No doubt it is priceless.

Give the Benefit of the Doubt, Don't Doubt the Benefit

Let's face it. We all have some degree of doubt. We live in an uncertain world that can breed distrust like rabbits spawn other rabbits. It's in our nature to be suspicious of the motives of others, some more so than others. No one can be sure about what another person intends in a relationship. Establishing a relationship puts us out there, making us vulnerable to the other person. But in a one-on-one relationship, both partners share that same risk.

This is where the idea of giving the benefit of the doubt comes into play. If no one were willing to give another person the benefit of the doubt, no relationships would ever be attempted, never mind be successful. It would be a lonely world for everyone if that were the case. In fact, it's not a stretch to say that all civilization would cease without the ability to give the benefit of the doubt.

Yet, there are so many people who, after seeking a relationship, begin to doubt the benefit of having the relationship. Why does that happen? There are a myriad of differing reasons that I've heard, but the overwhelming majority of them, when they are distilled down into their essence, is the lack of trust.

Building Trust

> *To be trusted is a greater compliment than being loved.*
> —George MacDonald

Trust—it's a fragile commodity. It takes a lifetime to earn and can take but a moment to lose. Yet, relationships cannot last without it. It's a commodity that does not transport easily; great care must be taken to protect it when shipping it to someone. That's why long-distance relationships must be made of sturdier stuff than a relationship with someone nearby. It's all about the fragility of trust.

It is not only fragile, but it can be elusive. Pulling trust out of the depth of life's sea is akin to snagging that storied but elusive blue marlin. Trust is both the essence and the energy of a relationship, but it isn't as easy to catch as it is to maintain.

Trustfulness indeed abounds in a child, but it's not a quality and endures to adulthood in many. A teen can be robbed of trustfulness in a flash, stolen away by a single careless act. Should the teen escape to maturity with trustfulness intact, an adult's world can quickly snatch it away as if it never was a quality they possessed.

Today's world paints a grim picture of relationships. Throw in the tendencies of an overthinker to mistrust either themselves or other people, and it's a wonder that any relationship can even start; so how can it last?

Well, it just so happens that we have a built-in desire to want to start and nurture relationships. This propensity for relationships persists in humans despite the odds stacked against relationship formation in our present society rife with ever-growing distrust. I've spoken enough about scripture's view of relationships in this book for you to know that scripture has something to say about this societal wonder, but for the sake of time, and since I've touched on it before, I'll let that rest here.

But since humans have this built-in programming to desire relationships, what must also be built into their psyche? Given the need for trust in relationships, there must also be an ability to rebuild trust. I say rebuild because it is evident that trust is a built-in feature for children. Young children trust implicitly, even those who develop rampant cynicism in adulthood. Children, who are more sheltered from society's distrust, retain more of this trust in maturity. But in most cases, trust is something that we have lost in some measure since our childhood.

Let's get to the subject at hand, then. How can we rebuild that trust in our relationships? I like to keep things simple because it is the best teaching method, in my experience, so let's just use an acrostic of the word trust itself to help us through it.

T-R-U-S-T: Take the First Step

I've alluded to this before, but to review, taking the first step is being the first to commit to something in a relationship. The very first step is the commitment to the other person. If trust is going to exist in a relationship, someone will have to commit first. It won't happen otherwise.

Give the Benefit of the Doubt, Don't Doubt the Benefit

What is a commitment? That's a fair question. Think of it as obligating yourself to another person. You are going into this relationship as if you owe something to the other person you intend to repay. We're not talking in a financial sense, but the obligation is in relationship currency.

A relationship is merely an establishment of a bond between two things. In chemistry, water is formed when hydrogen and oxygen start a relationship to share parts of themselves to create the necessary bonds.

Relationship currency is the sharing of parts of yourself with the other person to create one of the bonds necessary for that relationship. The idea is that the other person will then give you what is needed to start the relationship. Therein lies the risk, but someone must first step out on that proverbial limb. Still, the more you're willing to risk, the greater the bond can become.

If you enter a relationship unwilling to risk anything, no lasting bond will occur. It's simple chemistry in a relationship sense.

T-**R**-U-S-T: Responsibility and Reliability

When a relationship first begins, the bonds are weak. Even if you're willing to risk a lot, the other person may not be as willing just yet. More has to be done to strengthen the bonds and build trust.

The next step is to show that you are worthy of more risk. A solid way to do that is to do what you indicate that you'll do what you say and be there when the other person needs you to be there for them.

Doing what you say is taking responsibility for your actions. If there is a direct or implied agreement that you'll do certain things within this relationship, you do them as your responsibility, without fail. There will be times when this means giving up what we'd prefer to do for the health of the relationship.

When Jenny and I were first married, there were things that I liked to do that Jenny didn't enjoy. By the same token, there were things that Jenny wanted to do that I didn't enjoy. We had to learn to sacrifice our wants for the better of the relationship. I would do some of those things that Jenny enjoyed, and she would do some that I enjoyed. In many cases, what started out as a concession to the relationship became things that we learned to enjoy together.

We fulfilled our responsibility to each other in other little ways, like in the division of labor around the house. After a time, the little things we conceded to each other strengthened our bond to the point that we became very comfortable that we would always be there for one another. We had proven ourselves reliable partners to each other.

Of course, the division of housework doesn't apply in dating or relationships with friends, but the point is that there's always some small way to demonstrate these qualities to each other. In dating, a test of your responsibility is just doing what you say you will do. If you say you will meet at a particular time, be there at that time, not a half-hour late. If you say that you're going to do an activity that you know your partner enjoys, but you don't, do it anyway for the good of the relationship. If you do what you say you will do without fail, you're building reliability in your partner's eyes.

T-R-**U**-S-T: Understanding

Relationships require understanding. This is not understanding in the sense of knowing everything about someone. No one really knows everything about themselves. It is the kind of understanding that allows you to accept what you know or think you know about the other person.

I had mentioned earlier that Jenny has a very vibrant personality at times. This is the personality that I first knew when we began our relationship. Then, after a few months of marriage, I saw a change in her that can be described as becoming more sedate and reserved. At first, this change baffled me. I just knew that it was something that I did that caused the difference, but all along, she insisted that there was nothing wrong between us. It took a while, but eventually, I accepted the fact that my wife was different than me. I began to understand that our interactions would differ when she was in what I learned was her default personality. It wasn't that the exchanges were unpleasant; it was just that they were different.

Jenny's more vibrant personality is fed by positive emotions. She is vibrant when she is anticipating something with a measure of excitement. Her vibrancy is not exhibited as much when life settles down into the humdrum of life. When I understood that as the way her personality operated, the stress that it caused in our relationship vanished. My only regret is that I didn't come to this understanding sooner. Vibrant or not, this was my wife, and when I accepted that, our relationship grew closer because I stopped those mini-overthinking cycles and began to enjoy the person that she is.

Understanding is a commodity that is in short supply for most overthinking minds. This is because we get all caught up in ourselves when we overthink. It is a deadly thing to a relationship. The best thing we can do is to overcome the cycles and allow ourselves to truly understand our partners. If we do that, most of our reasons for overthinking vanish, and our relationships become much healthier.

Ann Landers wrote a very popular advice column for many years. One reason she became so popular was that she could distill very complex relationship issues down to their most fundamental parts and then help people with what she had learned about those parts. The following quote is how she defined a romantic relationship. I invite you to think about it without overthinking it.

> *Love is friendship that has caught fire. It is quiet understanding, mutual confidence, sharing and forgiving. It is loyalty through good and bad times. It settles for less than perfec-*

tion and makes allowances for human weaknesses.
   —Ann Landers

T-R-U-S-T: Satisfying Needs

The whole reason for a relationship is to satisfy your needs, whether they are social, emotional, spiritual, or, in some cases, physical. The problem with overthinking is that it tends to dwell on your own needs or deficiencies depending on the cycle type. Therefore, many times, the needs of a partner are overlooked. A relationship should be symbiotic, not parasitic in nature. In other words, if one part of a relationship is always giving but not receiving benefits in return, the relationship will either be a misery or a short one.

In a healthy relationship, both parties receive mutual benefit. One such relationship in nature is the clownfish and the anemones. Most of us are familiar with the clownfish because of the character Nemo in *Finding Nemo*, a Disney movie. The anemone is the flower-like animal with which clownfish spend most of their lives. The anemone has potent neurotoxins that can paralyze prey. Clownfish are immune to this toxin. The clownfish benefit in gaining protection from their predators and thus much longer lives. In turn, the clownfish benefit the anemone by driving away anemone predators, dropping food down to the anemone when they feed, and even secreting feces, which nourishes the anemone. Many scientists believe that the clownfish movement is beneficial to aid in water flow, bringing oxygen and plankton into the anemone's reach. The colors of the clownfish may also attract some other prey into the anemone's grasp. The clownfish and anemone thrive in this relationship because they both benefit.

Human relationships that are indeed symbiotic have the same effect on their partners. The partners both thrive and become better persons because of the relationship. This betterment is not an accident. We are designed to have relationships; only our faults, such as overthinking, prevent them from having their intended mutual benefit.

The provision of each other's needs can only occur if we understand each other in a relationship. Human relationships are more complex than the clownfish and the anemone. They are physically designed to benefit each other. Humans are socially, emotionally, spiritually, and, yes, in the realm of marriage and monogamy, are physically designed to benefit each other. These different aspects make the relationship beneficial for all our lives, but they also complicate relationships. The most essential elements are also the most complicated: social, emotional, and spiritual. These are the aspects of living that need the most attention.

So, to sum up this point, we need to meet the social needs of our partner and be their companion in life. The emotional needs are met by being a stimulator of positive emotions and the stabilizer of negative emotions. Spiritually, we need to complement and encourage each other. These points sound simple but are rather involved, and this book is not designed to address them adequately. The thing that you need to glean, though, is that you have something your partner needs; never forget that. That giving attitude in a relationship can form the long-lasting bonds we were intended to maintain.

T-R-U-S-**T**: Truthfulness Within

The most critical adhesive for a relationship is the trust that it engenders. But if you'll recall, we've touched on the fact that trust is highly fragile. The glue that holds trust together is truthfulness. Truthfulness is a quality that has to be worked upon constantly, for we all have the latent or active desire to deceive. Sometimes, we think that there is no harm in deceiving ourselves. Still, some of the most egregious errors we make in our decisions are because we have deluded ourselves into believing a fantasy or a falsehood that we wish to be true.

We do this for perceived self-protection, avoidance of uncomfortable reality, and self-advancement, to name a few reasons. Whatever the motivation, this self-deception hampers trust. If you don't admit who you are, how will you relate this valuable information to someone else? How can others understand you if you're constantly putting up false fronts?

Without truthfulness within, we cannot be wholly truthful with others. If we're not honest with others, the trust upon which our relationships are built can be likened to a house of cards. When the slightest of breezes comes our way in the form of the smallest of problems, our trust is knocked to the floor, and our relationship crumbles with it.

Actually, truthfulness within is more than just being who you authentically are. Authenticity helps build trust, but it doesn't complete the picture of who you are. Authenticity demands that we stand for the beliefs and values that define us and convey those honestly to others. It does reveal part of who we are through the façade we put up. Therefore, it can help. It's a start, a step in the right direction.

The trouble with merely being authentic is that it doesn't go deep down to the core of who we are. It doesn't reveal any deceptions you've convinced yourself of when you formed your beliefs and values. Authenticity shows the person you currently are, not who you are at the core. Some folks have lived so long under false assumptions and pretenses that they've buried the truth of who they are deep under tons of earth.

Truthfulness within is not a scan of your current condition; it's an excavation searching for the essence of your soul. The inner truth of who we are is not a reality some of us are willing to face. We cover it with layers of lies. All of us have something that is not pretty underneath all that pretense. This reckoning of the truthfulness within provides us clarity as to who we really are. It provides us with the anchoring point that will enable us to withstand the storms that come our way. Only once we have that kind of inner truthfulness can we begin again to make wiser and more fulfilling decisions.

Take inventory of your life. Are your current beliefs and values based on things you initially knew were fallacious but accepted anyway because of external influences or pressures? Everyone was born with the knowledge of the truth, the absolute truth, not somebody else's truth. The muddling of that truth brings all the internal conflicts within us. Exposing yourself to that inner truth can allow you to become a person who can sustain trust and, thus, a relationship. A person who can do that is not easy prey for overthinking.

Be Honest with Yourself and Others
❖◆♦

It's discouraging to think how many people are shocked by honesty and how few by deceit.
—Noel Coward

The quote above is playwright Noel Coward's observation of the effect of human society on humans. Human society has always been fraught with deceit. The ancient Greek philosopher Plato stated, "Honesty is for the most part less profitable than dishonesty." This reveals the core of deceit. Even in ancient times, deceit was viewed as a societal tool to better one's position in life. A tool is something to be used to accomplish a task. People routinely use deceit in society as a tool. The most obvious examples are politicians. Plato's younger contemporary and in many ways, his counterpart, Socrates, said, "I was really too honest a man to be a politician and live."

But deceit isn't only found in politics. It is all over society. It is detected in direct lies that intentionally alter the truth. It is discovered in equivocations, making indirect, misleading, or ambiguous statements designed to apply negative implications to people, institutions, or ideas or, conversely, to imply positivity upon fabrications. It is found in concealments that omit relevant information or behave deceitfully to hide damaging truth. It can be dug out of exaggerations of the truth that attempt to validate a false narrative and understatements that downplay the significance of truth. It is found in untruths, the use of truth selectively and out of context to misrepresent the truth. These are all common in society and show no signs of slowing their development and refinement in our modern society.

These tools are used in an attempt to avoid the consequences of misdeeds. They are used to protect interests in less noble engagements. They are used to make people look good despite the opposite being true. And yes, they are used in relationships to avoid confrontation or in an attempt to extend them when detrimental actions need cover. There is really no need to continue. I think we all recognize enough of these deceits as being prevalent in our society. It's the reason that we are numb to it in modern politics despite the flaunting nature of its use. Deception has become a cultural norm, an expected behavior.

Sadly, most couples today go into a relationship expecting or at least suspecting deceit. This is not a healthy starting point. Trust and deception don't mix. Our society has produced a multitude of overthinking minds, each trying to deal with the expected betrayals that we see are so commonplace today.

The good news is this doesn't have to be the case. A relationship can be a refuge from deceit; in fact, it should be. I'll double down; it must be for it to be a healthy relationship.

Authenticity

I realize that the chapter section on truthfulness was more conceptual than practical. This was done on purpose to have a concept to build upon. That concept is that we all have layers of deceit woven into our lives. We can blame this on society, but who makes up human society? It's individual humans; is it not? One realization that we need to come to terms with is that we, as individuals, are responsible for these layers.

The teaching of authenticity is a way to strip off one of these layers, namely, the most recent layer of deceit that we have taught ourselves. I did say that authenticity was a step in the right direction. So, to be practical, I'll need to explain how authenticity works and can be implemented.

Authenticity is defined in many ways in psychology circles. Still, the most representative of commonality of meaning is this definition: the quality of being genuine and true to one's own values. Another way to word it is to align your actions, interactions, and thoughts with your true values. The idea is to sync up your life with who you are. The contrast is not to portray yourself as actors might portray their roles. This thought aligns with an old mantra: "In life, everyone's an actor, but only a very few get paid for their roles."

Know Your Trends

The first step in determining your authentic self is to note how you react to specific daily activities and interactions. Did you like doing that or dislike it? Did anything give you a unique feeling of joy? Did anything sadden you, even slightly? Did anything make you feel tired or energetic? Jotting down these simple observations over a week can give you some insight into what you value and don't value. See how those observations hold up the following week. Are they the same? Did they change? If they changed, did you consciously change your reaction, or did they change naturally? If they changed naturally, what made them change? Were you tired or well-rested last week compared to this week?

Questioning yourself in this manner and writing down your observations can help you see your trends and how you are handling the circumstances of your life. It'll give you a snapshot of how you're viewing your life.

Once you have noted your reactions to things your life presents, try to identify the values they represent. The *Moving Beyond Overthinking in Relationships Workbook* has a section where you can jot down your reactions and provides a list of common values to assist you with this task.

Know What Improvements You Need

If you find that your documented reactions tend toward the negative side or your reaction notes don't indicate much joy or energy, your life choices don't match what you value. If you gather enough data to see what some of those values aren't or are, evaluate how to address those values either through a hobby or by finding more rewarding work. For example, if you find joy in being creative, working at a clerical job won't give you much joy.

When life choices don't match your values, you live a life that is not your own. It's time to see what the motivations were for the choices that you made. Was that motivation something that you really, truly value? Or is it a value you think you should have because you're emulating someone else? Were the choices made out of convenience, you know, the easy way? Were they made because you thought they might bring you success in how society views success? If they were made for any reason other than your values, those decisions are simply another layer of deceit in your life, and you're not living honestly.

Live with Integrity

Living with integrity means that you're living with a moral compass. Your decisions are guided by desires and a sense that what I'm doing is right. It is the sense that by doing this, I'm keeping myself a whole person; I'm not selling myself to the highest bidder. I'm not torn between desires and virtue. Integrity builds self-dignity in the right way.

With integrity, you don't hesitate to do the right thing, so you never have to second-guess yourself. The alignment between who you are, what you do, and what you believe is perfect.

How would you feel if, every day, you said what you meant, stayed true to yourself, not someone else, and behaved accordingly? Imagine the happiness and self-respect you'd feel! Being authentic to yourself is far less stressful than being someone you are not.

Don't Assume Negatively

Another old adage that comes to mind is a word-play on the word *assume*. "When you assume, you make an ass out of you and me." It holds true.

There is no profit in making negative assumptions, particularly about another person. We all make assumptions in the sense of supposing a thing to be true without proof. For example, a person who opens a retail store has to assume that nearly everyone will pay for the items they want. It would be silly to assume negatively in that general sense. However, the general assumption may not apply if the owner sees someone they deem *shady* entering the store. The owner might identify that person as a risk, a person to bear watching. That is an example of a negative assumption, but as long as there is no confrontation with the *shady* person, no harm is done. However, if we take the same example, but this time the owner asks the *shady* person to leave without actually seeing that person do anything amiss, then the owner assumes something to the point of accusation. The offended person has every right to seek legal compensation in such a case. So, you see, there is a big difference between making an assumption and interacting with a person based on that assumption.

Our interactions are really actions of sorts. Once you interact in any visible way, you're committing an act. If we assume the worst in people, sooner or later, that assumption will show itself in a related action or reaction. That is where you could be proven to be that ass that the adage talks about, and worse, you take another person along for the ride.

Manage Your Emotions

The dumbest things I've done were acting or reacting out of emotion instead of reason. The easiest thing to do for us is to let our emotions control our actions and reactions, but it's also the worst thing to do.

You might say, "But Kenny, since reacting with emotions is natural, aren't I being my authentic self when I do that?"

My answer to that question would be, "Sure, if you're real self is an irrational, uncontrolled and uncaring beast of a person."

Part of being authentic is to show our values. If you make decisions with your emotions, you're showing that you value recklessness. If you react with negative emotions, you indicate that you value antagonism. On the other hand, offering emotional control allows you to still have room to display the positive values you genuinely cherish.

Truthfulness versus Authenticity

Being authentic is a vital first step toward truthfulness. Practicing authenticity allows you to rid your life of pretense, a form of deceit. Pretenses will not allow you to practice truthfulness. But what is truthfulness if it's not authenticity? That's the question we will explore in this section.

First, let me give you an example of what it is not from history. When Israel left Egypt, they were led by Moses, who was led by God. Once they came into the land of promise, Joshua took Moses' place as leader.

Things were going well with Israel in their battles against the Canaanites while Joshua lived. Then Joshua died.

After a short time, the Israelites stopped prospering in the land of promise. They fell into a stagnant state. Soon, other people in nearby lands saw the opportunity to take advantage of this complacency. Little by little, Israel lost sovereignty in their land and were brought under the yoke of various nearby peoples. It was a time when Israel had no King or leader like Moses and Joshua to keep them faithful to the way God wanted them to live. As a result, God would raise up what came to be known as Judges in the land to lead Israel to victory over their oppressors. But once success was achieved, Israel would again fall back into faithless complacency, and they would be brought under bondage again. This cycle repeated itself all through the book of Judges. This phrase is seen a couple of times in the history of that time: "...every man did that which was right in his own eyes."

The problem with the Israelites of that time wasn't that people weren't being authentic. They were doing what was right in their own eyes, which is the basic message of authenticity. The problem was that different people were following different values, which changed with their circumstances.

Within the authenticity section, there was a section about having integrity. I'm not the only one who includes that stipulation when teaching about authenticity; it's a fairly common element to include. But why is that the case? Admittedly, integrity is not a value everyone has, so why zero in on that value when teaching about being oneself? It is because it is a value that implies that you also honor these values: moral stability, incorruptness, uprightness, and honesty. These traits were taken from Webster's Dictionary's definition of integrity. The last three, incorruptness (or incorruptibility), uprightness, and honesty, are all well-defined values that aren't subject to much change. They are appropriate, considering that the trait of moral stability leads the list of attributes. Integrity adds stability to authenticity, which isn't found within the idea of authenticity itself.

Stability is important. People from many walks of life have spoken of its importance. Here are a few of their quotes.

> *There is no coincidence that stability brings success, and success brings stability.*
> —Robert Green

Success to me is only two things: happiness and stability.
—Kehlani

It is important to find a place where you feel trust, you feel belonging and stability.
—Bojan Krkic

Always remember that the most important thing in a good marriage is not happiness, but stability.
—Gabriel Garcia Marquez

Marriage is gonna be your stability through everything.
—Miranda Lambert

People respond in accordance to how you relate to them. If you approach them on the basis of violence, that's how they'll react. But if you say, 'We want peace, we want stability,' we can then do a lot of things that will contribute towards the progress of our society.
—Nelson Mandela

Without stability, your values mean nothing; your authenticity becomes inauthentic.

Truthfulness then is when your values, the important ones that affect other people's lives, have stability. A person cannot derive their values solely from self, because every person has the possibility of changing their values depending on their situation. It can't be derived from society. Living in the past few years has proven how swiftly a society's values can change. The important values that make up truthfulness can only be derived from a stable source.

Some have appealed to something called Natural Law. Natural Law is a theory in ethics and philosophy that says that human beings possess intrinsic values that govern their reasoning and behavior. These values are universal and immutable. There is a measure of truth in that we all have a conscience that helps us determine right and wrong. But I part ways with the notion of each person's conscience being unchangeable.

To my knowledge, there is only one Being who is immutable: God. I'm not speaking of a god of the gaps as the Greek gods were, filling in where Greek knowledge could not take them. Not a god who is imagined to be just a like mankind, but superior in power. Not even the god that inspired the awe of ancient man, the unknowable numinous in their writings. But rather, the God of Scripture. That God is knowable, and is made known in Scripture. The God that is immutable—unchangeable.

Given that God is that only known source of immutability, the ultimate of stability, I appeal to the Scriptures, the Word of God, as the only stable source of truth. This then is where true truthfulness is found. The only source of truth that is truly stable in the entire world. A value system predicated on Scripture is the most stable value system possible.

Truthfulness vs. Authenticity

A person with truthfulness will never find their values to waver. The will be more stable than a rock in a relationship, but with much more personality. Good values such as creativity, assertiveness, excitement, or expressiveness are for the individual. These values add personal identity to a value system. These are the values that may change without detrimental consequences to a relationship. But the values that must not change such as honesty, contentment, sincerity and selflessness, these values must be taken from a stable source that can be referenced to ensure our adherence to them. These values form the cornerstone of our relationships. These are the values that need to stay true. Truthfulness then is seal of our trust, the commitment to our bond, the one foundation upon which trust can securely be built.

Communicate Clearly
♦◆❖

Don't Make Assumptions. Find the courage to ask questions and to express what you really want. Communicate with others as clearly as you can to avoid misunderstandings, sadness and drama. With just this one agreement, you can completely transform your life.
—Don Miguel Ruiz

Now that we understand how to rebuild trust and why that's so important, the next step is to avoid messing up all that work with poor communication. Ruiz is right; courage is needed to communicate clearly. None of us are perfect. Despite our efforts, it is impossible to completely fill that room for improvement. With imperfection comes the inevitable. Someone is going to screw up, and a conflict is going to emerge within your relationship. The closer the relationship, the more dreadful the conflict will seem.

By screwing up, I don't mean that an action or even an inaction always causes the conflict. The most common cause of conflicts in close relationships is misunderstanding. Somebody has again resorted to reading smoke signals.

Okay, now one or maybe both of you have misread something, and now there is that dreaded *something* between you and your partner. What happens next is the key to whether a nuclear detonation is imminent or the bomb squad gets there in time to diffuse the situation. It would be nice if an actual team of people could swoop in and do all the hazardous stuff in this situation, but in a relationship, you and your partner are the bomb squad or the culprit responsible for setting off the explosion.

Flight is not an option for either of you. Running from the bomb will only let it go off, and you both have to live with the aftermath of this explosion.

Fight is a terrible option because that means the bomb has already been triggered, and it will make a terrible mess.

The only reasonable option is to confront the bomb and deal with it. So, how does an actual bomb squad have the nerve to face a real bomb? Squad members speak of endless hours of training and research on every possible bomb configuration and type. They talk of endless hours of testing equipment. But in the end, they speak of the confidence that all this preparation gives them. They have confidence in their skills and confidence in their equipment.

One squad member spoke of something more. "We are all aware of the danger. In fact, we speak of it freely. It's hard to describe, but having confidence that you will get the job done doesn't take away the danger or the fear, but somehow, my fear enhances my confidence. I feel I can diffuse any bomb when the time comes"

Confident Vulnerability

Truthfulness with yourself and others gives you the confidence of your convictions. Just as all the preparation makes the bomb squad members confident, your faith in your values gives you enough confidence to follow your beliefs in all circumstances, even when trying to diffuse a relationship bomb. Only *trying* to be more confident doesn't work, especially at the moment. Confidence is not something you can turn off and on. You feel confident because you are at peace with the person you have become. True confidence is evident even when you face that bomb of hurt that could expose your weaknesses. Your truthfulness makes you believe you can diffuse any possible exposure to harm, even if it exposes your weakness.

At the same time, you are confident, and you are vulnerable. You take your vulnerability in stride because you know you will not betray the trust in your relationship. The more helpless you feel, the more your confidence rises to face it.

Therefore, beginning a conversation about the issue, no matter what it is, no matter how grave it appears, is not something you have to work up the confidence to do. The confidence is already there, ready to use.

I mentioned that Jenny's default mode is to be reserved. I had started to become aware of that when I sensed *something* was amiss between Jenny and me. She wasn't just reserved in her behavior; she was deliberately ghosting me. She remained unresponsive no matter what topic I'd try to bring her into a conversation with me.

I know women might be familiar with this within their relationships with men, but I was indeed in the dark about what the problem might be. I got slightly angry because of the ghosting and wanted to show that anger. However, I knew that acting out an emotion was undoubtedly not the way to get to the heart of the matter, and after a time, I really *NEEDED* to get this resolved. It was driving me crazy. Like a typical man, however, I didn't want to be the first to cave in.

Finally, I put aside my emotions and asked Jenny to join me in the bedroom. (We had children in the house at the time.) There, I laid bare all to Jenny, my emotions, and all my ignorance about what was happening between us. I did this with a confidence that I didn't know I possessed to that point.

Jenny started to cry. Apparently, I had been a terrible person. Then she related to me how I had said something hurtful to her.

I remembered having said it and thought at the time that I was just being funny. But Jenny didn't think it humorous at all. So, instead of arguing my point, I merely said, "I'm so sorry, Jenny. I'll try not to do that again, but if I do, call me out for it."

That is when we got to the good part and kissed and made up. We were Kenny and Jenny once more.

There will be times in any relationship when you're going to feel vulnerable to hurt. Having the confidence of your convictions can be just the tool you need to diffuse that hurtful bomb.

> *When we were children, we used to think that when we were grown-up we would no longer be vulnerable. But to grow up is to accept vulnerability...To be alive is to be vulnerable.*
> —Madeleine L'Engle

Navigating Conflict

Remember our bomb squad friend? One of the reasons for his confidence was the familiarity that he had with his equipment. This section aims to give you some equipment or tools, if you prefer, to assist you in diffusing your relationship bombs. We already discussed one tool, but it's worth noting here.

Practice S-L-O-W

You will feel stressed if you're about to deal with a conflict. This can signify that the overthinking mind might be about to cycle. This would not be a good time for that, so instead, stay in the present by taking a deep breath or two; this will allow your body to release the building pressure.

See your thoughts and label them. This will help distance you from the negative emotions that those thoughts might be harboring.

Now that you've distanced yourself from your thoughts open yourself to the present. Focus on your external senses, what they see, smell, and hear. Touch something if necessary to add that sense to keep you in the moment.

Once you are back in the moment, welcome the confrontation you're about to start. Use the confidence of your truthfulness and begin by using one or more of the tools below.

1. **Ask Consent.** When you bring up the conflict, don't just plow into it like a drunk driver on a freeway. Instead, you might ask, "I want to discuss an issue with you. Are you open to doing that now?" If they're not, don't push them into it. Try to get them to set a time when they have time to talk. Asking for consent demonstrates respect and encourages their collaboration with you.
2. **Practice Transparency.** Transparency here is revealing your inner state to others. Conflict is brutal for most people, so telling them it's not easy for you is okay. Convey what you're feeling by opening with that. You could also say what

you think this conversation means to your relationship. "I'm concerned that this has already damaged our relationship, which I really value. I want to clear the air and get things right between us." Practicing transparency can make you feel vulnerable. It reveals that the outcome and perhaps the other person matters to you—which means they have the power to hurt you. Disclosing this can calm their fears that the conflict will lead to you rejecting them. This honest opening up of yourself might make their position less rigid and allow them to listen more fully to you.

3. **Reveal Impact.** If the conflict centers on some incident or words spoken, reveal what impact that had on you. "When you teased me about ___, I felt ___." "When I did ___, I was ___." Fill in the blanks with the words or incident that caused whatever feeling you felt. Keep the first part objective, not subjective. Go to the actual action or comments; don't translate the first part into the emotion you felt. For example, don't say, "When you ignored me" as the first part because that's an assumption you made at the time. If your hypothesis is wrong, it could start another argument. You're only putting your feelings into how that objective thing, such as the person turning away, made you feel.

4. **Ask Curious Questions.** Ask questions to explore instead of assuming. What do they want most? What was behind the other person's comment or action? What kind of support do they desire? Have they experienced something like this before? What is the impact of this problem/conflict on them? What do they fear? What do they hope? Starting with questions opens the door to a common understanding of the situation, what's desired, and what's possible. Genuinely curious questions make the conversation about the essence of your relationship and solving a problem.
5. **Reflect Their Words.** Reflecting means repeating what the other person said. Don't embellish or attribute motives they didn't state; instead, summarize their words accurately. You might state: "What I think I heard you say is…." Ask them to confirm, correct, or reconstruct what you said to add to your understanding. A good follow-up question would be, "Is that the way you see it? Do you want to add anything?" When you reflect this way, you find out if you understood. You demonstrate that you listen well, hear the other person's words, and can hold them without distortion. If the person understands that they are being heard, it can diffuse tension in the conversation.

6. **Use the Power of "Yes, and…"** Within a confrontation, there will undoubtedly be points of contention, moments when the two of you don't see eye to eye about something. The point that both of you have is often valid from each of your perspectives. Instead of trying to force the person into seeing it your way, accept that their view is valid. Once they've expressed their view, use "Yes, and…" to initiate your view. This acknowledges your partner's view as being valid, thus increasing the possibility of acceptance of your view. It shows you were listening and encourages the partner to listen to you.

These are just a few techniques to help diffuse the bomb in your relationship. The concept behind each is to have an attitude of reconciliation, not confrontation, when a discussion about a conflict is necessary.

So what if you're not in a conflict, but your partner exhibits signs of a problem. Since you care for them, you want them to open up to you about it. The following section talks about how to really listen to them so that they'll have no problem opening up to you again.

Listen with Empathy

> *I like to listen. I have learned a great deal from listening carefully. Most people never listen.*
> —Ernest Hemingway

Like most writers, Hemingway understood the benefits of listening. Listening isn't something everyone does well. The Greek philosopher Epictetus said, "We have two ears and one mouth so that we can listen twice as much as we speak." It's a saying that has been used and paraphrased for centuries. Perhaps someone might have said a version of the phrase to you at some point. Not all of us speak a great deal, but I suppose we all hear more than we listen.

Hearing could be described as the passive process of taking in sound waves. We do that all the time, don't we?

Listening is an active process. I'm not talking about merely absorbing words or even the context of the words. Listening is more than just noting the feelings that accompany the word. To listen is to understand. There is a difference between knowing what a person is saying and understanding what a person is saying.

When you listen with empathy, you not only understand what a person is saying, you are putting yourself in the other person's shoes, so to speak. You're trying to comprehend their motivations for the message that their words are conveying, not with presumption, but with an observation of the tenor of their voice, the expression on their face, and the emotion in their eyes. When you focus in this way on the person and show interest in their message, you move from recognizing words to understanding the feelings and motivations behind them. This includes following up with questions if needed. It's also about knowing when to stay silent.

Empathic Listening is a compassionate process that calls for more than taking in someone else's words. You're actually conveying a message to that person as well. You're showing that you're concerned about them; their thoughts and feelings are significant to you, and you are willing to take the time to hear them out.

To the best of your ability, you become the other person. You are attempting to connect with that other person's frame of mind. Your goal is to try to help, not to assume things they are not saying, as so many overthinking minds like to do. So, instead of starting a thinking process about their message, you give them your undivided attention. Listen with your mind and heart open.

While you're listening, sprinkle in some communication, not with words, but with eye contact and nodding that you understand. If appropriate, take their hand if they're willing to give it. Be in that moment with the other person.

Don't be afraid of silence after the person seems to be done talking. Sometimes, a person needs to be heard or know you're there. They may be thinking about how to proceed or just need a moment of silence for reflection. Speak only when what you have to say is worth breaking the silence.

If you speak, speak to further understand. Paraphrase what was said to confirm your understanding. Be respectful in what you say and look for signs that the person wants to respond. Let them, as the initiator of the conversation, have the last word unless they desire a response from you. Be sensitive to their needs at all times.

This empathetic interaction will strengthen the bond between you and your partner. However, empathetic listening can be utilized with anyone who needs to talk. It will not only help them, it will make you a better person.

Make It Last
❖ ❖ ❖

Time is too slow for those who wait, too swift for those who fear, too long for those who grieve, too short for those who rejoice, but for those who love, time is eternity.
—Henry Van Dyke

It's fair to say this book has two parts. The first part dealt with overthinking almost exclusively, and the second part discussed relationships more than overthinking. Taken as a whole, it is my hope that the book has been helpful to you on both topics.

As a teacher, I understand that if something is truly learned, it will become an innate part of you. The knowledge gained will be there when you need it. That is why when I taught, I taught more in concepts than in rote learning. Likewise, I tried to convey my thoughts in the book in ideas. I didn't repeat things in a rote manner but instead tried to relate each point to the other points to build one idea upon another. The notion of using a companion workbook, the *Moving Beyond Overthinking in Relationships Workbook*, was to reinforce the ideas I related in this book by encouraging you to interact with those ideas in differing ways. I hope that some of these concepts might stick with you in this manner and thus help you going forward.

The goal of this book is two-fold, to let you get past or beyond the crippling habit of overthinking to a place where you can enjoy meaningful, lasting relationships. It wasn't meant to be a manual for marriage, but since marriage is a significant relationship, it was featured prominently. Nevertheless, the principles imparted within this book have a universal quality: they can assist you with any type of relationship, whether personal or business.

The first thing we want to do in this chapter is reinforce the concepts already taught that, if learned, can improve the quality of your life and your relationships. So, let's get on with the bolstering of the main concepts.

A Quick Bolstering

We spent a good amount of words on the first concept we covered together. The initial chapter's title spoke to it: *View Overthinking as a Dilemma, not a Definition.* One of the main problems I've seen with overthinking people is that they don't apprehend the severe dilemma that overthinking puts you in. They get that they overthink but don't understand what it does to them. If an overthinker believes that their habit is not a real problem, that is a problem within itself. The first chapter was, therefore, devoted to establishing that *overthinking is a huge problem.* It can lead to even more significant issues and is a killer of relationships. It was the only place to start in my mind. To use an analogy, a horse will not drink if he thinks he is not thirsty. In other words, people have to understand they have a problem before they can be motivated to act on it.

The second central concept was introducing the *SLOW method* to deal with the beginning moments of an overthinking cycle. If the cycle never truly starts, overthinking never really happens. Of course, there were concepts within that concept, but the acronym helps you to remember them. Can you remember them now?

Next, we talked about how to stop the habit of overthinking or ruminating. The main ideas here were *discovering your triggers and mindset and knowing gratitude's positive role.* All are related in that your triggers are caused by your mindset and that injecting gratitude into your mindset can eliminate many of those triggers.

TRUST was the next big concept. It is a necessary ingredient in a relationship and a deterrent to overthinking. Implementing the ideas of TRUST into your relationships is the first step in creating more intimate, lasting bonds. Again, there is an acronym to help you remember the individual ideas inherent within TRUST. A good bit of time was also spent here because of its importance.

Then, we attempted to understand the significance of *truthfulness.* We did this by exposing to you the deceit that is all of us and how truthfulness cannot exist with deception. Then, we defined and compared truthfulness to authenticity. Truthfulness includes what authenticity lacks: a stable foundation.

Lastly, we spoke about *communication*, what it is, and how to do it effectively. A particular focus was given to the listening aspect of communication.

This was very brief, I know, but I have treated all of these central concepts with care throughout the book. I just wanted to remind you of the basics before introducing the last concept.

Sincerity

Sincerity is an interesting word in the English language. It has substantial meaning in many aspects of life. It can mean you're guileless, having no deceit in your mind. It can mean that you hold honesty in great regard. It can mean that your intentions or motivations are pure. It also implies that you have gained freedom from hypocrisy, disguise, and false pretense. It says a lot about a person. To have this label applied to you is a high honor indeed.

You haven't read to this point in this book without having some sincerity within you: the sincerity of intention. You intended to complete the book when you started it and saw that intention through to the end. I congratulate you on the sincerity of your desire to finish the book.

But how does sincerity apply to the rest of your life? That is a question that we should all ponder.

Sincerity makes the very least person to be of more value than the most talented hypocrite.
—Charles Spurgeon

You don't have to have talent to be sincere. It's neither a question of intellect nor a question of will *per se*. It does touch on other virtues, however. It touches on honesty, motivation, and purity of intention. It also touches on something that is lacking, and that is guile.

Guile isn't used a whole lot in everyday vocabulary today. At its core, it's the intent to deceive. It is being double-minded to put on a front that makes another believe something you know is not true, complete with all the trappings of a true belief. You act and react as if this something is true. I've seen this play out in movie plots. A person might be selling that another person died to protect them from a threat to their life. They will openly grieve and mourn, all the time knowing that the person is actually alive. In this case, that is guile with an altruistic notion, but guile is rarely used in that fashion.

Guile is usually used for selfish reasons. It is more often employed to manipulate people. It is frequently utilized to make yourself look better than you actually are, either in ability or as a person. In either of those cases, guile is used to deceive a person into thinking of you more highly than you deserve. More importantly, guile is frequently used to deceive ourselves.

Many have vowed to follow a strict diet to improve their bodies. Yet, in the very moment that we make that vow, our mind is busy churning out ways to get that one craved dessert or comfort food. Still, we make the vow, relying on our willpower to see us through, yet we already envision ways to cheat on that vow. We are double-minded concerning the vow because it's not what we really *want* to do; it is what we *should* do.

You cannot allow yourself to do this when it comes to overthinking. You have to have sincerity of thought about the problem. You can't let a mental urge to survive. You must learn to hate the notion of overthinking to the point where it's no longer something you want to do. I should emphasize that your hate should only be directed toward the habit; don't transfer the hatred to yourself and start a different overthinking cycle. When the urge to overthink comes at the very onset of that first negative thought, revulsion needs to take hold of you that is so strong that your immediate reaction is to go SLOW. As you win these little battles, you will feel a rush of satisfaction that can further quell the hormonal drive to overthink.

I understand it is easier said than done, but that's the goal that needs to be set. That's the level of expectation that you should select, sincerely set, in your mind.

Although missing in many relationships, sincerity is the key to relationships. You have to sincerely believe that your relationships, especially that crucial relationship, whatever it may be, can be your refuge from the storms of life. It can be an anchor you can rely on to keep you steady. It can be your motivation for keeping everything else right in your life.

That is what my relationship with Jenny has been for thirty-six years and counting. Our marriage has brought us through all the rough patches of life. It has seen us through hardships and sorrowful walks of sorrow through the valley of death as precious loved ones are lost to this world and to us.

Not only has it been a refuge, it's been an anchor for us. No matter how crazy life gets, we never detour from our purpose. We rarely lose perspective; we can always count on each other.

And lastly, but perhaps most importantly, our bond has motivated us to strive to improve our bond.

Our marriage is a never-ending drive to be more than we were before we knew each other, to be one, in mind and soul, even as we have been for each other in body.

Do you sincerely want the kind of bond Jenny and I enjoy? If so, the bonus chapter is meant for you, the sincere seeker. It describes the essence of our bond and manifests the catalyst that allowed me to move beyond my overthinking dilemma.

Wrapping It Up

A sincere spirit is the only human quality that can provide a lasting result to any human endeavor. Curiosity, though it can be a trait that leads to discovery, cannot sustain the marching of time. Patience, though an admirable virtue, has its limits. It is not a virtue that we humans have in infinite supply. Though a divine emotion, love is not sufficient in humans to endure all things within ourselves. Too many times, we rely on a *reason to love* because we don't fully comprehend what it is to love.

But sincerity is a value that endures deceit since the presence of sincerity forbids the company of internal deception. It allows us to fully commit, and sincere commitments tend to last. Our founding fathers were passionate about establishing a nation free from tyranny where every man was allowed to live and worship as he chose. That ideal is still alive in many hearts, enduring nearly 250 years. It is imperfect, as all things created by humanity are. Still, the sincerity of heart and vision made an enduring thing out of something that previously had no existence in the history of mankind.

If you have the sincerity to practice the lessons this book provides, you can see a lasting transformation in your life, and I sincerely hope this is the case for you.

If this book helped you, please leave a review on Amazon. Your few sentences could be the encouragement someone needs to change their life.

BONUS CHAPTER: It's All about Relationships
A Faith-based View

Welcome to the bonus chapter. I've included this section in the book to provide a deeper understanding of what a relationship can be and really should be.

I don't want there to be any misunderstandings, so I'm letting you know up front that this discussion is going to be of a spiritual nature. It is man's innate nature that we can't see or touch, but all of us have been aware of it to some degree in our lifetime. Though it can be helpful, psychology can only probe so deep into the psyche of a human without considering the spiritual nature. In this section, we will explore humanity's spiritual aspect. To make the discussion more seamless, from this point on in this section, we'll refer to the psyche by the term used by Scripture, the soul.

It's All about Relationships

What is a soul? According to Webster in 1828, it is man's spiritual, rational, and immortal substance. But to further expand, it is the part of man that the Scripture sometimes references as the heart but never the brain. This is an interesting comparison because we understand that the heart supplies life to the body. There have been instances recorded where a body goes on living for a time, though the brain stops functioning. Undoubtedly, the brain is critical to the continued survival of the body, but the heart supplies life to the brain. So, if there is an organ that can be representative of the soul, it would be the heart.

Further, the Scripture says, "For the life of the flesh is in the blood." The heart, then, is the supplier of life. Therefore, in a true sense, the soul is the life of our body and spirit. It is the life of our immortality as well. It is the core of our existence.

This is an essential point because the soul communes with the spiritual realm. There is no physical organ that does so. This is why, to the naturalist, the spiritual realm can't exist. But I can sincerely say that I have experienced that realm. Therefore, I know that it exists.

Ancient humans were aware of the spiritual realm. The evidence for that is plentiful. It is found in the many temples and religious icons of antiquity. Many today try to explain it away as a social function or, as some have espoused, a mass delusion. But the findings of archaeology reveal something so innate within all men to cause diverse cultures all over the world to try to satisfy that *something*, that spiritual craving. Though all of them believed in something the Greeks called the Numinous, a holy Being that created great awe and fear, they settled for worshipping lesser gods, ones that they tried to make more "human" than the Numinous. Essentially, they were trying to bring their god into their physical world to make their god less fearful. To them, the Numinous was unknown. The Greeks even made a shrine to the *Unknown God* in Athens.

But the Numinous doesn't have to remain unknown. That is the wonder of the Christian faith. The Scriptures tell us much about God, the Numinous of the ancients. The Scripture tells how we can relate to Him as well.

Imagine, if you would, a Being who exists in eternity. A timeless Being that, at some point that we would call the long ago, before the universe came into being, existed alone—and yet not alone, for this Being had and still can act as three separate but unified parts.

It's All about Relationships

These parts function as if they were individual Persons, for indeed, they are distinct Persons, yet the Being is one. If you can imagine this, you have the beginning of the description of who the Numinous is.

With that in mind, we can conceive that this Being would have the most intimate of relationships among these three parts. This relationship would have a closeness that we cannot begin to understand with the social limitations of our present form.

This Being made a decision that the relationship this Being had amongst the three Persons was to be shared. The motivation for that can only be hypothesized, but perhaps it was because sharing the relationship would produce so much joy. This is put forth as a theory only because when humans share what we have, it gives us joy, and the Scripture tells us that we are made in the image of this Being, which we call God.

Let me inject that we are given the names of these three Persons in the New Testament Scriptures. There is God the Father, God the Son, and God the Holy Spirit, which can be shortened for brevity to the Father, the Son, and the Spirit. This is the Trinity of Scripture.

This decision began to be implemented with the creation of a man, Adam, by name. We know that Adam and God had a relationship from Scripture, but it wasn't the same as the relationship between the Father, the Son, and the Spirit. The man wasn't one with God; therefore, God and Adam's relationship was limited.

God, of course, understood that, but he had something else in mind. He initiated the next phase in His plan by creating a woman out of the body of Adam. Adam called her name Eve. It was here that the most holy of bonds on earth was established. As Adam and Eve were of one flesh, so would the bond between a man and a woman be. Genesis 2:24 states, "Therefore shall a man leave his father and his mother, and shall cleave unto his wife: and they shall be one flesh." That was the design of what we now call marriage.

This is as close to an emulation of the bond within the Trinity that can be accomplished in our current human form. You know that Jenny and I have achieved a very rare closeness in our relationship, but it doesn't compare with the relationship within the Trinity. Nevertheless, our relationship has benefitted from that Trinity relationship, and the next step that God implemented is how that is possible.

God's plan continued to unfold. Adam and Eve were good; that's what God called them and His creation. Because they were good, they could commune directly with God. This is strongly implied in Genesis 3, where the Voice of God, probably a reference to the Son, was walking in the garden where Adam and Eve were. Adam and Eve had an intimate relationship, perhaps as close as any man and woman had ever had, and they had close communion with God. However, the relationship between God and man was not as close as God desired to share. It could not be since God is indeed one Being, and Adam and Eve are separate beings.

To occupy him, God had given Adam the responsibility of the care of the Garden of Eden. This was before Eve was created. He also gave Adam one command. "Of every tree of the garden thou mayest freely eat: But of the tree of the knowledge of good and evil, thou shalt not eat of it: for in the day that thou eatest thereof thou shalt surely die." God had made Adam with an eternal soul, so dying in Scripture doesn't mean a cessation of bodily functions as we associate with death today, but it did involve that. Death is a separation. Adam, at that time before Eve was created, had only one connection to lose: the relationship with God. If Adam ate of that one tree, he would be separated from God, and his body would begin to deteriorate and die as well. Adam knew that disobedience to this command would end his relationship with God. This one command initiated the next phase in God's plan.

This phase of the plan was a painful one for God, Adam and Eve, and us today as well. Adam and Eve were given free will. They didn't have to obey God. They could disobey. And disobey is what they did. Eve was deceived, the first deception in history, and Adam knowingly and willingly joined Eve in the eating of the forbidden fruit. Humans have had a lust for the forbidden fruit ever since. In that moment, God lost the relationship with Adam and Eve, Adam and Eve lost their relationship with God, and Adam and Eve lost some of the closeness of their relationship. The deterioration of their bodies was no doubt a secondary loss to that first human couple. Human life was all about relationships from the beginning and has been ever since.

God is holy, and that disobedience and the desire to be disobedient to God have separated us from a holy God. But God still longs for a relationship with mankind despite man's disobedience, man's sin against Him.

God made some temporary provisions for humans to maintain a relationship with Him. The first provision was the conscience, the moral compass God gave us. It directs us toward Him when it is untarnished. But the conscience is temporary because it becomes tarnished at a young age, some younger than others.

The ensuing overture you see from God is with Abraham. God and Abraham formed a close bond, so much so that Abraham was called a friend of God. This bond created a covenant with Abraham, whose offspring became Israel. Israel was given more in the way of temporary provisions in the giving of the law and worship through blood sacrifices of animals. But Hebrews tells us, "it is not possible that the blood of bulls and of goats should take away sins." These were temporary practices pointing the way to one event.

> *For God so loved the world, that he gave his only begotten Son, that whosoever believeth in him should not perish, but have everlasting life.*
> —John 3:16

This verse is probably the most well-known portion of Scripture, and for good reason. The Triune God gave a part of Himself, namely the Person of His Son, to the world so that God walked among men as a man.

This is God's permanent solution to the *great relationship problem*. Romans 5:8 tells us more, "But God commendeth his love toward us, in that, while we were yet sinners, Christ died for us." If you're unfamiliar with the name Christ, it refers to the Son. God showed forth His love with this gift. This is why Adam's sin was part of the plan. How else could God show us just how much He loved us? By giving a very essential part of Himself to die, He demonstrated His commitment to having a relationship. It's the "T" in *TRUST*, if you will. God has made the first move of commitment. All we have to do is to take that first step toward Him in acceptance of his first step. There is no fear of rejection since God has already made His intentions known. This is how we can take that first step.

> *That if thou shalt confess with thy mouth the Lord Jesus, and shalt believe in thine heart that God hath raised him from the dead, thou shalt be saved.*
> —Romans 10:9

Saved? Save from what? You'll be saving yourself from the penalty of rejecting God's gift. You'd be saving yourself from refusing to have a relationship with the only Being that can take away the curse of death, which is separation from God forever. If you think that's not so bad, consider this. God is the only source of goodness in this world. Without God, no goodness will befall you in eternity. The Son, known as Jesus on earth, said this to those who had never accepted His gift. "I never knew you: depart from me, ye that work iniquity." (Matthew 7:23). It's all about relationships, and it always has been.

> *The fear of the Lord is the beginning of knowledge;*
> —Proverbs 1:7a

The quote above tells us how to begin to have knowledge. This is speaking of any knowledge worth having. But it's also talking about the first step in having a relationship with God. To have a relationship with anyone, you must take time to know that person. It's no different with God. Ancients referenced Him as the Numinous. They had a dread of Him. It is, at least, the correct attitude to have toward God. God is a holy God with terrible power. However, the fear of the Lord doesn't have to stop at a dreadful fear. To have a relationship with God, the fear of the Lord must progress into knowing Him. God addresses this in Proverbs 1:24, where He says, "I have called, and ye refused." God clarifies who it is that is refusing His call in verses 28 and 29, "Then shall they call upon me, but I will not answer; they shall seek me early, but they shall not find me: For that they hated knowledge, and did not choose the fear of the Lord." Those who do not choose the fear of the Lord are the ones about whom God laments their refusal of His invitation.

Do you remember what I said about how an overthinking mind has to treat overthinking? I'll quote myself here. "You have to learn to hate the very notion of overthinking to the point where you it's no longer something you want to do."

To establish a relationship with God, this is what you have to do with all the things separating you from God. Those things you know aren't right deep down inside, yet you do them or think about them. You have to put away your pride and submit yourself to God. You have to hate the very notion of doing anything that would offend God and, in sincerity, turn to the God that's inviting you to know Him. It's all about relationships; it always has been.

That's the hard part; now, here's the good part. God's influence on your life in the form of his Spirit speaking to you about the Son, within that deep down part of your soul, will guide you into a depth of relationship that you've never known before.

It's All about Relationships

Faith is needed for a relationship with God, but it's not blind faith. It has tangible substance as the Spirit works in tandem with your soul. As your faith strengthens, you can clearly see the reliability of God. You come to know that the Son understands you as no one on earth can because he knows your inner soul and what living as a man on earth is like. There is no lack with the Father because he supplies all your needs, whether they be physical, emotional, or spiritual. Jesus said, "I am the way, the truth, and the life," in the book of John. He is truth, the essence of truthfulness. "Jesus Christ the same yesterday, and to day, and for ever" (Hebrews 13:8), so the foundation of your relationship is sure. Each Person working in concert builds your trust in this relationship better than any human who has mastered *TRUST*.

What is the secret of our relationship, Jenny and I? It's not of our own making. God has been there in both Jenny's life and mine, cementing our union. God has given us a oneness that I can't begin to describe in words. That oneness came from the Spirit's edifying influence individually, which in turn helped us edify each other. The building up of each other brought that closeness to us.

It's why we've navigated difficulties that might have overwhelmed most unions. It's the source of our extraordinary love for each other. Not to mention, my relationship with God is what pulled me out of my dilemma. I simply trusted what the Voice of God told me to do: take a step of faith.

The best news is that you can have this relationship too and much more. God is so infinite that you'll never stop learning about Him as your relationship progresses. It is no wonder that the Psalmist proclaimed, "Great is the Lord, and greatly to be praised; and his greatness is unsearchable." Yes, God is unsearchable because you'll never be able to fully explore the infinite God, the awe-inspiring Numinous, yet He is not unknowable.

The relationship I am trying to describe in this book is too vast of a topic to cover in this chapter. Though I wanted to do it justice, I believe an entire book might not be able to cover it all.

If you would be interested in a book about this special relationship and what it can bring into your relationships, let me know by indicating your interest when you leave your review. If enough people are interested, I'll attempt to write that book.

Resources

Ackerman, C. E., MA. (2023). How to Live in the Moment: 35+ tools to be More present. *PositivePsychology.com.* https://positivepsychology.com/present-mment/#:~:text=Living%20in%20the%20present%20moment%20means%20letting%20go%20of%20the,you%20breathe%20is%20a%20gift.

Amaha. (2023, September 1). The science behind overthinking. *Amaha.* https://www.amahahealth.com/blog/science-behind-overthinking/

Cpi. (2016, October 12). 7 Tips for Empathic Listening. *Crisis Prevention Institute.* https://www.crisisprevention.com/Blog/7-Tips-for-Empathic-Listening

Cuncic, A., MA. (2023). How to be more present. *Verywell Mind.* https://www.verywellmind.com/how-do-you-live-in-the-present-5204439

Definition of overthink. (2023). In *Merriam-Webster Dictionary.* https://www.merriamwebster.com/dictionary/overthink#:~:text=%3A%20to%20think%20too%20much%20about,I%20went%20to%20New%20York.

Glowasz, M. (2022, April 2). What does 'Embracing Uncertainty' Really Mean? - Predict - Medium. *Medium.* https://medium.com/p/10dd9fa72fda

Gupta, A. (2022, April 29). Are you stuck in the vicious cycle of overthinking? It's risky, warns an expert. *Healthshots.* https://www.healthshots.com/mind/mental-health/heres-how-overthinking-can-impact-your-overall-health/

Hill, Linda (2023) *Recovery from Relationship Anxiety and Overthinking.* [Kindle]. Independently published.

How to stop overthinking your relationship. (n.d.-b). Greater Good. https://greatergood.berkeley.edu/article/item/how_to_stop_overthinking_your_relationship#:~:text=Thoughts%20like%20these%20can%20arise,into%20what%20psychologists%20call%20rumination

Resources

Hyland, M. (2023, April 13). *5 ways to discover your authentic Self - SparkVision*. SparkVision. https://sparkvisionnow.com/5-ways-to-discover-your-authentic-self/

Immel, S. (2021). 6 Techniques To Constructively Navigate Team Conflict. *eLearning Industry*. https://elearningindustry.com/techniques-to-constructively-navigate-team-conflict

mindbodygreen. (2021, July 1). *How Are The Mind & The Brain Different? A Neuroscientist Explains*. Mindbodygreen. https://www.mindbodygreen.com/articles/difference-between-mind-and-brainneuroscientist#:~:text=So%20what%20exactly%20is%20the,mind%20also%20changes%20the%20brain.

MindTools | Home. (n.d.). https://www.mindtools.com/ay30irc/authenticity

Muñoz, A. (2022). *Stop overthinking your relationship: Break the Cycle of Anxious Rumination to Nurture Love, Trust, and Connection with Your Partner*.

Mutualism: eight examples of species that work together to get ahead. (2021, September 17). [Video]. Natural History Museum. https://www.nhm.ac.uk/discover/mutualism-examples-of-species-that-work-together.html

Njorge, A. (2023, May 12). How to eliminate uncertainty in your company 1 email at a time. *Inc.com*. https://www.inc.com/magazine/202303/allan-njorge/how-eliminate-uncertainty-in-your-company-one-email-at-a-time.html

O, A. (2023, March 2). *Research based leadership development - people acuity*. People Acuity. https://peopleacuity.com/is-vulnerability-the-new-confidence/

Stress symptoms: Effects on your body and behavior. (2023, August 10). Mayo Clinic. https://www.mayoclinic.org/healthy-lifestyle/stress-management/in-depth/stress-symptoms/art-20050987

Teachout, K. (2023). *Overcoming overthinking: The Complete Guide to Calm Your Mind by Conquering Anxiety, Sleeplessness, Indecision, and Negative Thoughts.*

Team. (2022, October 12). *What Causes Overthinking And How To Overcome It?* Refocus. https://refocus.com.au/what-causes-overthinking-and-how-to-overcome-it/#:~:text=The%20roots%20of%20overthinking%20can,common%20contributors%20to%20excessive%20thinking.

Therapy, M. O. (2021). Overthinking and anxiety: why do I overthink everything? *My Online Therapy.* https://myonlinetherapy.com/why-do-i-keep-overthinking-and-how-do-i-stop/

What are anxiety disorders? (n.d.). Mind. https://www.mind.org.uk/information-support/types-of-mental-health-problems/anxiety-and-panic-attacks/anxiety-disorders/

When overthinking becomes a problem & what you can do about it. (n.d.). Houston Methodist on Health. https://www.houstonmethodist.org/blog/articles/2021/apr/when-overthinking-becomes-a-problem-and-what-you-can-do-about-it/#:~:text=%22Overthinking%20can%20affect%20how%20you,daily%20stressors%2C%22%20explains%20Dr.

Where there's smoke, there's a message. (2018, June 13). Davidson Institute of Science Education. https://davidson.weizmann.ac.il/en/online/sciencepanorama/where-theres-smoke-theres-message#:~:text=Smoke%20and%20fire%20signals%20were,transmitting%20messages%2C%20even%20complex%20ones.

Made in United States
Troutdale, OR
10/01/2024